THE LABOUR OF SPIRIT

THE ITALIAN LIST

ALSO FROM **THE ITALIAN LIST**

Edited by ALBERTO TOSCANO

Hamletics
MASSIMO CACCIARI
Translated by Matteo Mandarini

Self-Portrait in the Studio
GIORGIO AGAMBEN
Translated by Kevin Attell

Name and Image
GIANNI CARCHIA
Translated by Matteo Mandarini

The Twilight of Politics
MARIO TRONTI
Translated by Matteo Mandarini

As Cruel as Anyone Else
ANGELO DEL BOCA
Translated by Richard Braude

Feminism in Revolt
CARLA LONZI
Edited by Luisa Lorenza Corna and Jamila M. H. Mascat
Translated by Luisa Lorenza Corna, Matthew Hyland, and Cristina Viti

The World Machine
PAOLO VOLPONI
Translated by Richard Dixon

The Soul of Brutes
CARLO GINZBURG

The Idea of World
PAOLO VIRNO
Translated by Lorenzo Chiesa

Primo Levi
MARCO BELPOLITI
Translated by Clarissa Botsford

This Body That Inhabits Me
ROSSANA ROSSANDA
Translated by Richard Braude
Edited by Lea Melandri

The Golden Horde
Edited by NANNI BALESTRINI by PRIMO MORONI
Translated by Richard Braude

MASSIMO CACCIARI

The Labour of Spirit

An Essay on Max Weber

TRANSLATED BY
MATTEO MANDARINI

LONDON NEW YORK CALCUTTA

This book has been translated thanks to a translation grant awarded by the Italian Ministry of Foreign Affairs and International Cooperation.

Questo libro è stato tradotto grazie a un contributo alla traduzione assegnato dal Ministero degli Affari Esteri e della Cooperazione Internazionale italiano.

Seagull Books, 2025

First published in Italian as
Il lavoro dello spirito. Saggio su Max Weber

First published in English translation by Seagull Books, 2025

Paperback ISBN 978 1 80309 514 1

Hardback ISBN 978 1 80309 513 4

British Library Cataloguing-in-Publication Data
A catalogue record for this book is available from the British Library

Typeset by Seagull Books, Calcutta, India
Printed and bound by Hyam Enterprises, Calcutta, India

Contents

Note on the Translation

While lexical choices are singularly decisive in philosophy, Cacciari's word choices demand particular attention. Particular words, everyday words, return again and again in his writings, arriving drenched in meanings accumulated across many Indo-European languages. They end up operating as concepts gathering together resonances through their theoretical echoes to other texts, diverse traditions, frameworks and disciplines, across various cultural practices and discourses. Take, for example, the noun *valore*, which one would typically translate as 'value'. Included in its meaning, sometimes implicitly, sometimes not, is that values are given, they do not exist outside of a process of *valuation*. They are thus linked to a *practice* of valuing performed by a subject that seeks to impose a scale of values. As Cacciari writes in *Hamletics*, 'Value must indeed *value*; an impotent value ceases to exist.'[1] The echo of Friedrich Nietzsche's notion of will-to-power should be heard loud and clear (as well as Max Weber's Nietzsche-inspired 'The "Objectivity" of Knowledge in Social Science and Social Policy'). It is not always possible to show in English the relation to value and to the will-to-valuing that Cacciari deploys throughout the text, so I have had to resort to less gainly ways to show that connection, for example, when translating *farsi valere* as 'asserting itself', I have also added the original in square brackets. In more complex cases, I have had to include a translator's note. For example, I have translated *valere-potere* as 'count/possess-power' and added a note to show how Cacciari's coinage combines 'to have value'—in the sense of 'to count'—with 'to have power to', as well as 'to be capable of'. In all cases where *valore* or its derivatives appears, I have tried to signal this in one way or another.

1 Massimo Cacciari, *Hamletics* (Matteo Mandarini trans.) (London: Seagull Books, 2023), p. 17.

Cacciari finds a variety of idiosyncratic ways to signal the importance of etymology, the pregnancy of meaning of specific words in his writing. The text is replete with foreign words, particularly German and Latin. He does not translate these because there is a sense in which he wants the reader to go and research the terms, to seek out their multiplicity of meanings that remain operative, acknowledging that no single Italian (or, in our case, English) word could faithfully render them. To that extent, the failure of translation—as well as its necessity—is asserted in advance. That the word is being used in an unusual way is sometimes evident from the way it pulls one up in a sentence, where it seems to play a different grammatical function than would be expected of it. Sometimes he does so through simple italics, as in the case of *decidere*, 'to decide', from the Latin *decidere*, also 'to decide', which can be broken down further into *de*, 'off', and *caedere*, 'to cut', to give us: 'to cut off'. So 'to decide' is to determine by an incision that separates. But more typically, Cacciari hints at his unusual use by hyphenation: '*inter-est*', '*con*-science', 'com-pared', 'contra-dicting', etc. I have occasionally unpacked this in the notes, but I have chosen not to burden the text with too many notes. So whenever this curious hyphenation takes place, the reader should be aware that the—typically—Latinate roots are being highlighted as central to the conceptual articulation underpinning the arguments.

Notes that end with the attribution [Trans.] are mine; the rest are translations of Cacciari's.

I

THE LABOUR OF SPIRIT

The *System of Science* was called upon to open itself to a world of unlimited potentiality: Western philosophical thought became *scientific* thought, able to *comprehend* within itself the power of modern science in its inextricable unity with Technology. The realization of such a world clearly presents itself as an infinite task and mission—since, for the scientific *ethos*, it is *intolerable* to not realize what it has *projected* in thought. The world is no longer a perfectly harmonious classical *kosmos*, nor is it a Christian *saeculum* in whose End one can have *certain faith*. The world is what science *does*, the goal that its operation attains and overcomes time after time. Hence, the System of Science demands *permanent revolution*: the self-consciousness it assumes in the period straddling 1789, from the Enlightenment to Idealism, generates the 'great transformation', understood in its essentially cultural-anthropological sense; every 'state' has value only insofar it already contains energies for its overcoming; its power is as effective as the manifest potentialities for its self-overcoming, which emerge from within. Thus, each 'state' configures itself in accordance with its material and formal principles as a *state of exception*; none could establish itself as paradigmatic, pretending to contain the unstoppable *becoming-world* of *scientiam facere* (making knowledge). Every 'state' is an exception insofar as it *exceeds* the preceding one and insofar as, in its current form, it never re-presents itself (this possibility *must* specifically be excluded). What eternally repeats itself will be the exception itself; what eternally persists is continual change. The strictly economic is a dimension of such an overall *forma mentis* (more than a mere 'worldview'). Marx understood this perfectly—his self-proclaimed 'materialist' disciples will not.

This *becoming-world* [*farsi mondo*]—of which the System of Science constitutes a representation, insofar as it is conscious of itself, that is, insofar as it comprehends itself philosophically—is the work of a *labour*. And the form of that labour cannot but be as revolutionary as the Age it inaugurates. That is, it must be *absolutely free labour*, for any servile characteristic would conflict *radicitus* [radically] with the meaning of the 'great transformation'. In the Age dominated by the *forma mentis* of the great transformation, every form of 'commanded' labour cannot but end up being *impossible*. For this reason, Nietzsche speaks of the proletariat as the 'impossible class':[1] the freedom the proletariat possesses to perform its labour is mere appearance—it is nothing but the possibility of transforming itself into a servant. But in the new Age, this condition is unsustainable, it results in a contradiction that is destined to explode. We might then say that the only 'logically' possible labour in the contemporary world—one that is coherent with the Scientific mission to open onto unlimited potentialities—is spiritual labour, *geistige Arbeit*. Spirit, Geist is the God that animates from within human *operari*,[2] the Spinozian *Natura naturans* become history and destiny, infinite creation, *self-cause*. The form of human labour must correspond to its image. Philosophical labour, *accomplished* in modern science, tolerates no judges standing above it, and so it becomes the paradigm of the epoch's *spirit*. Hence, its form imposes the revolutionary path towards the liberation of labour tout court. The forces that re-act to this destiny will necessarily end up being devoured by the fire that bursts from the mouth, the *logos*, of Geist. Or rather, the devouring fire is Labour itself, for Hegel as well as for Marx.

---

1 'Der unmögliche Stand'. Friedrich Nietzsche, *Daybreak* (R. J. Hollingdale trans.) (Cambridge: Cambridge University Press, 1997), pp. 125–27. The ignominy of being 'thus used', and the consequent invitation to *flee* from the world that imposes such an 'impossible' and to transform themselves into 'free emigrants in the grand style'. [Translation modified]

2 The Latin word *operari* has multiple meanings: 'to labour', 'to toil', 'to work', 'to devote oneself', 'to perform (a religious service)'. [Trans.]

This was the rose that was supposed to blossom from the rose of the present.[3] The *geistige Arbeit* creatively proceeds from the bloody crucible of the Revolution. From the System of Science proceeds that of Freedom. The epoch of the 'great bourgeois' is dominated by this idea. This is not utopia—it really does accompany the assertion of the socio-economic system destined to become world [*farsi mondo*]—if anything, it is religion. Fundamental aspects of its religious nature can then be found in the most radical critics of the bourgeoisie: it is also because the bourgeoisie is believed to have betrayed those ideas (a betrayal deemed necessary, inevitable) that its domination had to be defeated. This domination is intolerable as it is self-contradictory; more than that, it is *impossible*: to want to dominate *living* labour is like wanting to command Spirit itself, to want to impose oneself upon its actual and perennial *incarnations*! How could the bourgeoisie fall into such a contradiction and presume to establish its dominion over it? How could it be that the 'final cause'—which had given rise to the *universal Mobilmachung*, the 'great transformation', and so the establishment of the *geistige Arbeit* of which scientific labour is the paradigm—ended up being subordinated to and dependent upon economic ends? What caused such a heterogenesis of ends? Critical-revolutionary thought responds to the question, explains the 'scandal', as follows: wanting to establish freedom upon the System of Science is to stand the world on its head, reversing the real dialectic. In the same way that *scientiam facere* was the product of historical, social and economic conditions, so it is with the process of the liberation of

3 In the preface to *Elements of the Philosophy of Right*, it is reason that blossoms in the cross of the present, since it is *reconciliation* with actuality, and hence the preservation of subjective liberty in what is substantial. Philosophy is 'its own time comprehended in thoughts', which means that never will the concept be able to comprehend what *has yet to be*. Here is the difference not only between Hegel and the 'Left', but also with Fichte. However, the entire revolutionary process that follows Hegel *depends* upon Hegel's key concept of the conciliation of actual and rational, since only *Wirklichkeit* is actual, which is to say that the product of the *ergon*, of human action, is *factum* not *res*. Hegel, *Elements of the Philosophy of Right* (Allen W. Wood ed., H. B. Nisbet trans.) (Cambridge: Cambridge University Press, 1991), p. 21.

labour, the process of the real affirmation of the *geistige Arbeit*. Its subject, its real *hypokeimenon*,[4] could not be *Geist*, but would instead be commanded labour itself, once it had become conscious of its own impossibility. In its conciliatory nostalgia, the 'great bourgeois' dialectic had been unable to grasp the radicality of the contradiction that characterized its epoch; indeed, the form of the social relations of production, which characterize political structures themselves, contradicted that original 'final cause', reducing the *permanent revolution* to an indefinite increase in the material wealth produced and to continual technical and organizational innovation. Prometheus unbound by the revolution is once again chained within a hierarchy where, for the first time in the history of civilization, the dominant values (and *value* [*valore*] is only ever what actually counts [*vale*], that demonstrates power) are economic ones.[5]

The epoch of the *Bürgersinn*: the dramatic passage from modern metaphysics (the system of the rationalization of the image of the world) to contemporary *universal mobilization*—the epoch characterized by the *idea* of conciliation between the economic-political system and freedom, in view of the universal establishment of the *geistige Arbeit*—does not end with a sharp divide between the death of the 'heroes' (Hegel and Goethe) and 1848. Not because that idea continues to perform simple ideological functions of mediation and compromise, but because it is only within it that fundamental factors of the domination of the social form of capitalist production can be *conceptualized*.

---

4 This Aristotelian concept means 'what under-lies': in Aristotle's *Categories*, it refers to that about which one is speaking, its 'object'; but the idea of 'under-lying' is what influenced the Latin translation of the term: *subiectum*. In the *Physics*, it is the 'substrate' underlying physical change; and in the *Metaphysics*, it is 'substance'. For a useful discussion, see Barbara Cassin, Emily Apter, Jacques Lezra, and Michael Wood (eds), *Dictionary of Untranslatables*: *A Philosophical Lexicon* (Princeton, NJ: Princeton University Press: 2014), pp. 1070–72. [Trans.]

5 See, in this regard, the fundamental works of Louis Dumont, *Homo Hierarchicus* (Mark Sainsbury trans.) (Chicago, IL: University of Chicago Press, 1970) and *Homo aequalis* (Guido Viale trans.) (Milan: Adelphi, 2019).

To proceed indefinitely, the system of permanent revolution cannot but establish itself on the unlimited productivity of living labour. The energy that moves it is not material. Its fundamental production consists in self-reproduction through the diverse forms in which it manifests itself. The commodity, in its determinacy, is nothing but a moment, a manifestation of the Absolute, something that is abstract in its very materiality. It does not count for itself but only insofar as it contains the necessity of its self-overcoming. Its appearing must fade without delay. It must not *insist* on being, but rather it must, in a sense, live for its own death, thereby revealing the immateriality of its own essence. The tendential uprooting of wealth from all earthly 'immobility' is a consequence of this dialectic, which is nothing but the *extremely concrete* content of the Hegelian dialectical form. According to its *concept*, capitalism is essentially *financial* capital, because the passage through the determinateness of the commodity is only conceivable in it as the *now*, the uncapturable *nyn*. The productive system understood in its complete form, *en-ergon*, whether perfect or in action, is that of money from money. This *idea* is the Spirit of the system, the meaning that stirs all its determinations. In the same way that the value of scientific enterprise in the variety of its manifestations consists in *power* in itself, in the power to overcome all obstacles to its *augmentum*, so what constitutes the foundation of the capitalist system and of its power is not its production of commodities as such, but rather the production of their ceaseless *consumption*.

The idea of the *geistige Arbeit*, of a labour always reaching for the not-yet, that doesn't want to understand itself in the light of an End, that is hostile towards all spatial and temporal determinations, no longer appears reconcilable with the *Philosophy of Right* in all the versions of it that idealism had produced: from those still characterized, in the Kantian manner, by the form of the *ought*, right up to Hegel's version. Within the limits of such a philosophy, it seemed that only determinate sovereignties, accomplished forms, could be recognized and always in relation to a national *ethos*. The *spiritualization* of living labour contradicts all of this.

Nevertheless, it must demand a Right to the extent that it expects to be universally recognized. In any case, can there be a *rootless* Right? There can, but only in the 'deified' form of the contract,[6] where the relations between political powers themselves are conceived within its order and subordinated to it. The contract ceases to count [*valere*] as that which regulates relationships between private interests; or rather, it ceases to count [*valere*] as an *instrument* of regularization, to establish itself as the foundation of the only possible Order within the epoch of ceaseless transformation. Above the contract, a transcendent sky of universally 'human' categories that share its ahistorical nature and are fully available for all applications is allowed to persist. In addition to subsuming the regularization of civil society within different countries, the net of the *lex mercatoria* stretches over international political relations themselves. This 'universally human' has nothing in its abstract form that contradicts the 'universality' of 'human rights'. But in order to count [*valere*] in the same way as the former, the latter too would have to be fitted into the positive form of the contract, becoming a *norm* of international Law positively recognized and applied. That is, those very 'human' ends of solidarity, assistance, support for the weakest, etc. would need to end up being nothing more than contained in the contract. Even *com-passion*, in order to count [*valere*] effectively, needs 'contractualizing'.

The *Bürgersinn* was unable to foresee such a *destiny* for the epoch, despite having comprehended the fundamental dialectical form *ab origine*. The net of contracts, the undefinable set of private regulations that admit of no 'beyond' themselves, would have appeared to the 'great bourgeois' as a sort of manifestation of 'radical evil': the Evil that expresses itself as soon as the desire for the good of the other (the essence of justice for Aristotle) appears inconceivable other than as the application of a contract, one that is normatively guaranteed, and that reflects, as is its nature, the interests of both parties. The sin is not so much in doing

---

6 On the 'universalization' of the form of the contract and it juridical and political consequences, see Guido Rossi, *Il gioco delle regole* (Milan: Adelphi, 2006); and the vast output of Natalino Irti, in particular *L'età della decodificazione* (Milan: Giuffrè, 1999) and *Un diritto incalcolabile* (Turin: Giappichelli, 2016).

evil as it is in radically subordinating the good to contractually established private interests. If a subject is unable, for whatever reason, to enter the form of the contract, he or she will also be unable to claim any right. Only those who participate in it are free. Of course, the universality of Order is unable to consider contingency or fortuitousness, which stem from the formidable inequalities in starting points of the contracting parties, neither can it shoulder cases that over the course of time can limit or strengthen the power of the one or the other. The State of Law is the State that deems the pure form of the contract to be *above* it; the very idea of justice is reduced to such a form. Only those who respect it, who 'keeps to their end of the bargain', are just. The political regime that safeguards the contract and sees in it the foundation of all well-being or public *eudaimonia* is 'justified'. The power of the State is subordinated to the contract, that is, it counts [*vale*] to the extent that it guarantees the process of contractualization of every social and political relation.[7] The *philosophy* of Right is accomplished and ends here, for no logical passage can subsist between the juridical form of the contract, which regulates relations in civil society or in the 'commercial state', and the constitution of the political relation, that of citizenship. Moreover, the mission of philosophical labour, which interpreted *scientiam facere* from the perspective of just such a passage, also ends here. To conclude, here is that subsumption of the Political,[8] of political *culture*, by the Economic that decrees the end of the bourgeois age.

---

7 From this perspective, one might develop Schmitt's reflections on the 'value' of the State of Law in his early text. See 'The Value of the State and the Significance of the Individual' in *Carl Schmitt's Early Legal-Theoretical Writings* (Lars Vinx and Samuel Garrett Zeitlin eds and trans) (Cambridge: Cambridge University Press, 2021), pp. 163–242. Today that State can represent its laws as 'just' only to the extent that they express the *sovereignty* of the contractual form. Only in this way does the Norm crosses over into the empirical world.

8 The 'Political' translates *il Politico*, which can mean 'the Political' as a concept, as in Schmitt's *The Concept of the Political*, or 'the politician'. When the choice of *politician* rather than *political* seems clear, I shall write *Politician*. I shall retain the capitalisation in both cases to indicate that the ambiguity of the term should be borne in mind. [Trans.]

Weber's critical reflections appear in these decisive years, and it is in light of these that we must reflect anew on the present. The leap that occurs with the 'great transformation' is radical and irreversible, but it is necessary to 'depict it' with Machiavellian realism in its contradictions, not as an inexorable destiny that could only be overcome by another leap, this time entrusted to pure revolutionary will or to the 'spirit' of Utopia. It is necessary still to discuss the *geistige Arbeit*. Scientific labour, while operating exclusively in the net of the technico-economic system, at the same time, can only demonstrate its productivity and creativity if its autonomy is guaranteed; an autonomy that can always venture to the limit of self-referentiality. The very process of specialization is also the mark of this necessary abstraction from the exclusively economic end pursued by the system of social production. In some ways, scientific labour continues, consciously or otherwise it matters little, to liberate dependent and commanded labour. This can be understood as corresponding perfectly to the system's needs, but such a correspondence must each time be 'contractualized' or risk the outbreak of ungovernable social contradictions.

We find here the second indispensable dimension of the *geistige Arbeit*, the political one. The Political can certainly also be expressed as contestation of the primacy of the Economic, whether that contestation is founded on utopian ends or, whether—in line with the *forma mentis* of the epoch—it advances the demand for a technico-rational foundation of its power within an economic dimension. Nevertheless, there remains a Political necessity *immanent* to the system. This is a necessity that is even more cogent than in any other epoch and derives from the form that labour assumes in the present. Labour that is *in any case free* in becoming-world can also be forced to subordinate itself to the form of the contract; but it will never be able to accept an Auctoritas as 'naturally' superior to itself. It can accept an economic subordination, not a *spiritual* one. The individual is here always in a position of the *superiorem non recognoscens* (recognizing no superior). It believes itself to always be *pars senior* (sounder part). For this reason, the primacy of the Economic, in the forms it has assumed in this epoch, needs to flank the scientific *geistige Arbeit* with the 'spiritual' labour of the Political, that is, with the construction of a political Authority that, together with the capacity to guarantee the supreme power of the contract, knows how to obtain from the multitude of individuals the recognition of the congruity of its command with the demand for the inalienable freedom that agitates each of them. Weber believed that only a democratic-parliamentary regime would allow the (relative and always in question) success of this exercise of highest alchemy. He nevertheless was entirely aware that the 'conciliation' between the individual demand for freedom and political Auctoritas could also be realized through demagogic-plebiscitary logics: the multitude of individuals can come to feel itself to be 'recognized' by *dictatorship* more than it can through any form of parliamentarianism. The problem for Weber consisted in the fact that a form of Auctoritas would have, in any case, to assert itself in an inherently problematic nexus with the hierarchy of values of the epoch, one clearly dominated by the Economic. The universal net of contracts not only remains entirely powerless to confront the great international crises (they are *always* located on another scale from the *ordo oeconomicus*), but also, according to its very principles, it can only safeguard the contracting parties with a degree of efficacy—beyond these limits, it appears to be undermined by an inherent, underlying contradiction: its inability to 'internalize' within its Order *the* problem from which the entire movement of the epoch issues, namely, the demand for a conciliation between individual freedom and the political system. Not only does the Order of the net fail to assume a properly *katechontic* (restraining or withholding) value in relation to the dynamics of the technico-economic *Gestell*,[9] with their

---

9 The concept of *katechon* was revived by Carl Schmitt, who draws it from St Paul's Epistles to the Thessalonians, depicting a historical and spiritual power that 'restrains' the Anti-Christ. See Carl Schmitt, *The Nomos of the Earth in the International Law of the Just Publicum Europaeum* (G. L. Ulmen trans.) (New York: Telos Press, 2004); Massimo Cacciari, *The Withholding Power: An Essay on Political Theology* (Howard Caygill intro., Edi Pucci trans.) (London: Bloomsbury: 2018). For a different reading of the *katechon*, see Roberto Esposito, *Two: The Machine of Political Theology and*

incessant, every-increasing generation of contradictions and inequalities. But precisely thanks to Order's very successes, it also convinces the individual that the radical demand for freedom that moves her and agitates her will never be recognized. The profound frustration that this generates (envy, resentment, hatred—all the 'cold passions' typical of Nietzsche's 'last man') tends to discharge itself, at least to begin with, on political institutions and their representatives, denouncing their corruption, incompetence, their lack of authority. It will, however, be very difficult to put a stop to it on this level; it is difficult to think that radical doubt won't 'mature' of its own accord, *sponte*, if that demand for freedom (whose ultimate meaning resides in the idea of the *geistige Arbeit*) *is ever able to be satisfied* in the context of the logic of the system as a whole.

It is this issue that the vocational politician, the responsible politician, is called upon to respond to. With the waning of the *Bürgersinn* age, disenchantment and renunciation must not lead to the fatal error of confusing that waning with the death of the Political. With the end of bourgeois age, so too perhaps has ended the *structuring* turn of the religiously founded ethic at the origin of the 'great transformation'. But this one cannot thus assume that the problem of political Auctoritas has been resolved. In the same way that the polyarchy of individual interests in 'civil society' lacks self-regulating mechanisms by which to organize itself, the same is true in the international arena, where powers are always, in every case, driven by meta-economic ends. If it is the economic Order that dictates the new hierarchies of value, it is unable—according to its very principles—to internally resolve the idea of *geistige Arbeit* from which those very hierarchies are born. Spiritual labour, which today can assume the shape of scientific and political action, means, in essence, *liberation from all commanded labour*. What is needed is a

---

the Place of Thought (Zakiya Hanafi trans.) (New York: Fordham University Press, 2015). On *Gestell*, see Martin Heidegger, 'The Question Concerning Technology' in *The Question Concerning Technology and Other Writings* (William Lovitt trans.) (New York: Harper Torchbooks, 1977). [Trans.]

Political able to represent such an idea *within the capitalist system*; a political Authority that is able to 'convince' that such an idea can be pursued. That it is a real possibility insofar as it is immanent *to the dominion of the commanded form of labour itself*. Capitalism cannot help but *enact* [*agire*] such an idea. It can 'save itself' as a system, that is, believe and make believe that it can advance infinitely, only by *becoming political*. Should the terms be reversed? Rather than the Political being destined to be subsumed by the Economic, is it not the reverse, a full 'politicization' of the process of production and accumulation of wealth? Can only an effectively sovereign Auctoritas guarantee it? Economic *power* cannot express itself in all its force simply by believing that the science and technology put to work by the mass of employed labour can harmonize thanks to invisible hands. Without political authority, the immanent contradictions of the relations between these systemic dimensions will check its very power. Contemporary capitalism, in the competition between the different areas in which it manifests its dominion, needs Empire. *Imperare*:[10] effective command, at once *present* and indication-promise. The Political is not the past of capitalism, on the contrary, it could be its future—but only in the form of Empire and the *polemos* between imperial spaces. Here, there is continuity and difference with Weber's reflections.

To render the individual 'indebted' to the indefinite progress of the system, political Auctoritas must be turned into an indispensable structuring function. No simplification, no reductivism are conceivable here. And within these links, strictly properly *religious* motives will certainly return. The reason for this is already clear in Kierkegaard in the decisive years of 1847–48, in pages that Löwith rightly places at the end of his epoch-making anthology, *La sinistra hegeliana* (1960),[11] drawn from

---

10 The word *imperare* means 'to rule', but in the Italian the reference to *impero*, 'empire', is evident. [Trans.]

11 Karl Löwith (ed.), *La sinistra hegeliana: Testi scelti* (Bari: Laterza, 1960), pp. 469–78. [I have been unable to trace this passage to any of the English editions of *Purity of Heart*—Trans.]

Purity of Heart Is to Will One Thing. In him, everything begins with the radical *decision* between the individual of civil society and the Singular.[12] The system is always *tyrannical* insofar as it excludes the authentic *exception* that the Singular alone can express. Nothing could be further from politics as the *new religion* invoked by Feuerbach. Early Christianity's merciless war against all *religio civilis* is revived in Kierkegaard. However, he grasps the necessity contained in Feuerbach's motto: the Political cannot resolve itself in the Economic, for it to 'save itself' it will be forced to assume a religious timbre. Of what will the Political need to convince that new, emergent multitude that Hegel called *Pöbel* or rabble (completely removing, however, the *Roman* meaning of plebs)? That the dominant system pursues the idea of *equality*, that it constitutes an immanent logic of the system. This, Kierkegaard states, is logically *impossible* because with human means one can only create differences and inequalities. The idea of equality assumes a meaning of its own only within a meta-political, religious setting. According to Kierkegaard (and in this he appears extremely close to Tocqueville), this is true also for the idea of freedom.

Equality and freedom form, on the worldly plane, an insuperable contradiction—a contradiction that can only be conciliated through the term 'fraternity', a *Christian* fraternity. But 'fraternity' cannot assume any meaning within the immanent order of political space, whether in a Machiavellian or Hobbesian sense. Yet no order, no hierarchy is conceivable in the contemporary world that fails to recognize such ideas and that is not *believed to* be pursuing them. It is illusory to imagine one can govern masses *put to work* simply through kings, generals, popes

---

12 *Singolo* means both 'singular' and 'individual' and is used to translate Kierkegaard's *den Enkelte*. Douglas V. Steere's translation of Kierkegaard's *Purity of Heart Is to Will One Thing* (New York: Harper Torchbooks, 1956) renders this as the 'solitary individual', whereas Howard V. Hong and Edna H. Hong in their translation *Upbuilding Discourses in Various Spirits* (Princeton, NJ: Princeton University Press, 1993) render it as 'the single individual'. I have followed Cacciari's Italian, rendering *il Singolo* as 'the Singular', which rings strangely but involves less redundancy than the extant translations and whose strangeness serves to signal that it is a technical term. [Trans.]

and Jesuits, through programmes informed by a purely worldly logic. A form of the Political that presents itself in the form of the *boss*—a figure that even the capitalist always wants to or must distance himself from—is impossible. On the contrary: the Political counts [*vale*], which is to say maintains effective *power*, precisely by *realizing* the idea that no Boss is given in the system; that the system functions truly by progressively eliminating all inequality. This end is utterly impossible and yet it is indispensable to affirm it, not only to justify the existence of the Political but also to determine its very efficacy. As Kierkegaard concludes, if with the Reformation everything appeared to be religious but rather was political, today everything wears the mask of the political and is destined to exhibit its religious nature. Only in this form will it be possible to still place politics 'in command'.

Had Weber read these pages of the author of *Either/Or*, he would perhaps have considered the tendency as characteristic of anti-capitalist ideologies that were inevitably produced by the development of the system itself. This, however, would have been a very reductive reading. Not only does the political organization of the *Pöbel* need a *faith* of a religious type, it is the Political itself, without which the capitalist order is utterly 'unsavable', that is called upon to represent ends that in *no way* belong to the rational-worldly origins of its modern form. The Political must become its *simia* (ape), not to persist in being Political, but so that the system as a whole endures. For Kierkegaard, this is perhaps the clearest sign of the anti-Christic character of the epoch: equality and brotherhood, which are only conceivable within the order and in light of the relation between the Singular and God, are transformed into a mission of the economic-political *Gestell*; or, today, we should perhaps say of the Politico-economic incarnated in a polyarchy of Empires. If history does not end here, it must be because it is still depends upon the energy contained in the *geistige Arbeit*, in its *conatus* to resist as a power autonomous from its economic, political and religious subsumption.

II

DISENCHANTMENTS

Scientific and political labour are both *intellectual labours* and, together, they represent the *hegemonic* forms of labour within the Modern. A dual form, *dissos logos*, always on the point of being resolved into abstract separation, inner sundering. An *Ent-zweiung* (splitting) that is to be recognized and *comprehended*. We shall see how. The great Weberian lectures compose a 'cycle',[1] which faces this same problem head-on. For Weber, the discussion of both the dimensions of intellectual labour, like the question concerning their possible 'agreement', must be carried out in radical opposition to a position, a *Stellung*, 'which normally provokes extremely negative reactions nowadays' towards the 'process of intellectualization to which we have been subjected for thousands of years'.[2] We shall see who the representatives of such a position are, which will enable

---

1 The history of the two lectures, originally published in two separate little books in July 1919, and then in two different volumes of the *Gesamtausgabe*, is described in all the recent editions of the texts that are fundamental for the understanding of our epoch. The first was held in November 1917 and may have been repeated at the start of 1919. The title given to the cycle in its first Italian edition (1948), which contained an important introduction by Delio Cantimori discussing the general content of the cycle of lectures organized by the Freistudentische Bund, *Il lavoro intellettuale come professione* (Intellectual labour as a profession), is, for reasons I shall go on to explain, an extremely pertinent title precisely due to its extremely problematic character. It is important to note that in the time between the two lectures the Empire collapsed, which made rethinking the Political as a whole an absolutely urgent question.

2 Max Weber, 'Science as a Vocation' in *The Vocation Lectures* (Rodney Livingstone trans., David Owen and Tracy B. Strong eds) (Indianapolis, IN: Hackett, 2004), p. 12. Almost all quotations from this edition have been modified to reflect the Italian translation of Weber's lectures that Cacciari quotes from. [Trans.]

us to situate Weber's own position historically. We can, however, already assert that the antagonist-interlocuters who Weber most wants to engage with are not intellectual or academic circles, they are above all youth and student movements. It is their fate that causes the most anguish to the great intellectual. It is the youth that one must summon back to a *reality principle* with great urgency and with all necessary *pathos*. Their ruination, beyond that of the War, coincided with the entire culture that he wished to represent. Max Weber shows himself to be an authentic, if unheeded, pedagogue, in some ways the heir to that voice of the *Bildungsbürgertum* (which at that time may have already been powerless) represented by Schelling on 29 December 1830, in the very same Munich, who told the students in revolt: 'Control yourselves . . . '

It is easy to grasp this sense of mission that Weber feels weighs on his own scientific labour. It is more difficult to grasp the origins and foundations of his critique. One can already grasp the depth of it from the preceding quotation. The process of rationalization buries its roots in the very *princìpi* of the history and thought of the West. Although these princìpi are not themselves the object of theoretical consideration—as they are in Nietzsche and will be in Heidegger—Weber's historico-sociological analysis explicitly relates to them. For Weber, modern rationalization inexorably *incarnates* the original foundations of the idea of *philosophy* or *episteme*, and hence so does the European idea of *science*. To oppose the process of intellectualization would, ultimately, mean rejecting this very idea. Is this in the name of a romantic *Weltanschauung*, of a *Bildung*, of an education or forming of humanity as an integral personality, un-alienated from professional specialisms? Not at all. The authentic Romantic has nothing to do with such reactionary utopias. In many ways, the foundational presuppositions of Weber's disenchantment might be found in Romanticism's quintessential philosopher, Fichte.[3]

3 'Thus, the growing process of intellectualization and rationalization *does not* imply a growing understanding of the conditions under which we live. It means something quite different. It is the knowledge or the faith that *if only we wished to understand them, we could do so* at any time. It means that in principle, then, we are not ruled by

Over and above the evocative tone, the 'aura' that envelops the term 'disenchantment', what precise meaning should we give it? That the objective appearance, the being *Gegen-stand* of reality no longer 'enchants' us. That it is impossible to think a *thing in itself*. That it is impossible to think of anything that is not *ipso facto* a thought, a *positum* of thought. The 'I' opposes itself, in itself, only to itself—and it is tasked with comprehending and overcoming such an opposition. Which is to say, it must grasp nothing but itself in the other, freeing itself of its estrangement. Humanity will no longer fear being crushed by a nature-other-than-itself [*natura-altra*]. Humanity's products will no longer present themselves to it in this form: 'Humanity, you will no longer need to fear being crushed by things that are your products.' If this still happens today, it is precisely science—and the doctrine that teaches its significance and measures its scope, the *Wissenschaftslehre*—that demonstrates what power human reason has to emancipate itself from every material chain, from all natural dependencies. The *labour* of reason consists in submitting to itself 'alles Vernunftlose',[4] all that which presents itself as 'without reason', the immediate *non-'I'*. Such a liberation is today *in potentia*—but,

---

mysterious, unpredictable forces, but that, on the contrary, we can in principle *control* everything by means of *calculation*. That in turn means *die Entzauberung der Welt* [the disenchantment of the world].' Weber, 'Science as a Vocation', pp. 12–13. Knowledge—*or faith*, adds Weber!—that the 'I' constitutes the centre of a circle with an infinite radius, and that the *will* that animates it (*nota bene*: the *primacy* of pro-jectual will, is a paradoxical revisiting of Aristotle's *proairesis* in Schopenhauerian-Nietzschean key), will be sufficiently strong that in principle no achievement will preclude it, constitutes *the* fundamental philosophical problem that Weber confronts. It is precisely this that compels us, if it is correctly understood, to the Romantic-Fichtean reference beyond any purported 'Romanticism'.

4 Johann Gottlieb Fichte, 'Erste Vorlesung' in *Einige Vorlesungen über die Bestimmung des Gelehrten* (1794) [English translation: 'Lecture I: The Absolute Vocation of Man' in *The Vocation of the Scholar* (William Smith trans.) (London: John Chapman, 1848)]. See Cesare Luporini, 'Fichte e la destinazione del dotto' in *Filosofi vecchi e nuovi* (Florence: Sansoni, 1947); Claudio Cesa, *J. G. Fichte e l'idealismo trascendentale* (Bologna: Il Mulino, 1992); Marco Ivaldo, *Libertà e ragione: L'etica di Fichte* (Milan: Ugo Mursia Editore, 1992).

here, *potential* [*in potenza*] means that the 'I' already in itself possesses all the *energy* required to realize it. For Fichte, this certainly does not mean that humanity can *become God* but that it has the *duty* to free its path to approximate that End, liquidating all impediments that restrain or arrest it in its pursuance of the *infinite* actualization of its divine nature. That this is within its power seems to him already to be certain. Just as science *disenchanted* of the necessity that our being-there [*esserci*][5] should *depend* upon a *thing-in-itself*, so is practical-political action *disenchanted* of all Authority that presumes to impose itself on the freedom of the 'I'.[6] The doctrine of science, ethics and philosophy of right form an indissoluble unity of theory and practice. Philosophy is completed in the *System of Freedom*.

To harken back to Romanticism to contest the process of rationalization and disenchantment is, therefore, the index of a particularly reductive interpretation of the political meaning of *Romantik*, if not one that is utterly mistaken.[7] Yet the misinterpretation can be easily explained,

---

5 *Esserci* is quite literally 'to be there', in the everyday sense of 'I'll be there'. It also happens to be the Italian translation for Heidegger's *Dasein*, which, though in ordinary German often simply means 'to exist', literally means 'being there'. This seeks to capture the fundamental trait of that being who is 'thrown' into the world, which we ourselves are. Heidegger uses *Dasein* to escape the metaphysical, sociological, anthropological and other assumptions contained in the notion of the 'human subject'. [Trans.]

6 These central themes of the theoretico-practical link upon which the entire *Wissenschaftslehre* are constructed, are also expressed by Fichte in all their power in the *Contribution to the Correction of the Public's Judgement on the French Revolution* of 1793 (Jeffrey Church and Anna Maria Schön trans) (New York: SUNY Press, 2021).

7 I consider Carl Schmitt's idea of 'political romanticism', from his 1924 book of that name but conceived during the catastrophe of the First World War, to be extremely reductive, which is to say, to be an 'ineffective expression' incapable of identifying the relation between *occasio* and effect, and hence, is unable to act upon the world. Nothing is further from Fichte than occasionalist flights 'from the domain in which conflict unfolds, that is, from the domain of "the political" into a higher domain.' *Political Romanticism* (Guy Oakes trans.) (Cambridge, MA: MIT Press,

because the rationalization posited by Fichte asserted as its intrinsic *duty* (a *Sollen* immanent to the historical process, not a 'duty' that presumes to impose itself upon that process by force of moral imperatives external to the forces that act within history) to realize itself in that System of Freedom. But now? The true operation of disenchantment that Weber pursues is not so much turned against the naive opponents of the process of rationalization, it is rather critical of the idea that *doing science*—its *Haltung*, its concrete mode of being and of operating [*operare*], the effective and productive doing of scientific research, *scientiam facere*, in its peculiar traits that are irreducible to classic *theorein*[8]—can manifest itself according to universal ethical and political ends, that it contains within itself the end of the establishment of the Kingdom of Freedom. An end, *nota bene*, that contained nothing in its beginnings that was fantastical. Instead, it presumed to found itself on the very presuppositions of the intellectualization of the world, on the millenarian principle that supported the thought of the West: that is, that all things are knowable and, as knowable, controllable; that reason can do what it wants, which is to say, that it has no limit if not that which each time it reaches historically and defines in the course of its development. The real object of Weberian disenchantment is the connection or 'harmony' between the character of science, as *scientiam facere*, and the Fichtean *duty* of establishing-realizing the System of Freedom, the teleological comprehension of the *Scientific* hegemony of the West through ever greater specialisms in its very articulation. To disenchant the disenchanted, here lies the original and paradoxical core of Weber's discourse.

Scientiam facere has a constitutive link to the Protestant ethic—from which stems, through various threads, all the greats of classical

1986), p. 159. It is true, however, that Schmitt tends to make a sharp distinction between Fichte and the Romantic. This, in some ways, is also the case for Croce, who is himself prone to reduce the *Romantik* to irrationalism.

8 See Alexandre Koyré, 'Les philosophes et la machine' and 'Du monde de l'«à-peu-près» à l'univers de la précision' in *Études d'histoire de la pensée philosophique* (Paris: Gallimard, 1981).

idealism—and such a link, already the object of the famous 1904 text,[9] remains implicit and underpins Weber's entire analysis: the ethic of the 'I must' means 'to have to *perform* [*operare*]'; one unconditionally obeys the call, *Ruf*, of God by carrying out with utter seriousness one's profession, *Beruf*.[10] Labour par excellence, however, *in majorem gloriam Dei*, cannot but have a *social* character, ending up being maximally productive, *effective*, for the entire community. Which is to say, showing itself not only through singular 'subdivided' professions but, far more so, as the *set* of those forms of doing *and knowing* that only synergistically give rise to technical-scientific progress. However, it is *pure delusion* to think that *scientiam facere* displays intrinsic factors that can connect its idea to that of the System of Freedom, which is to say, to a perspective of overcoming the dominant conditions of estrangement and dependency within the contemporary social form of production. It is even more illusory to suggest that it can 'govern, *Beherrschung*, life', and constitute the

---

9 There is an immense literature on what Troeltsch called Weber's 'great work', *Die protestantische Ethik und der Geist des Kapitalismus* (*The Protestant Ethic and the Spirit of Capitalism*). See the important collection of essays edited by Constans Seyfarth and Walter M. Sprondel (eds), *Religion und gesellschaftliche Entwicklung* (Frankfurt am Main: Suhrkamp, 1973). Naturally, the fundamental role of the Reformation in the process of secularization of European society had already been underlined by all post-Hegelian thought, building on that of classical idealism. It is enough to think of the works of the Bauers and the Ruges, from which that of Marx himself derives in this respect. Without a doubt, the author who has more profoundly investigated the relationship between the 'bourgeois world' and Christianity from the philosophical perspective is Karl Löwith, beginning with his fundamental *Von Hegel zur Nietzsche* (1939); see *From Hegel to Nietzsche* (D. E. Green trans.) (New York: Columbia University Press, 1964).

10 The inner polarity of *Beruf* remains, nevertheless, evident. On the one hand, it must define itself in professional forms, while on the other, it refers to that absolute 'exception' where the Eternal calls the Singular to testify to it beyond all ethical codes. In other words, their remains within it an irresolvable contradiction between the ethical dimension and the religious dimension. See Mario Miegge, Lilia Carusi Corsani and Ugo Gastaldi, *Protestantismo e capitalismo da Calvino a Weber* (Turin: Claudiana, 1983).

path able to guide it towards *eudaimonia*. Nietzsche's demolition of such illusions is taken by Weber to be *definitive*.

Weber's debt to Nietzsche is in no way limited to this *pars destruens*. His entire discourse on the *professions* takes up the profound *logico-philosophical* dimension of Nietzsche's thinking.[11] It is precisely science in its necessary articulation into specialist professions and competencies that shows the impossibility of a knowledge integral to the thing, a so-to-speak *holistic* comprehension of the *Sache*. Neither is it the *business* of science to furnish such an understanding. Science is articulated positively in a series of particular *perspectives*. And the more the scientist is absorbed in investigation exclusively according to her perspective, the more will her work be effective, and the better will she show herself capable of fulfilling her duty and obeying her 'calling'. This structuring of scientific *operari* makes it logically inconceivable that it could have anything to do with ideas of salvation, freedom and happiness. The question of life as a whole, in its significance with respect to its End, but also as in Fichte's *Gemeinde der Ichen*—which is to say, in its intersubjective character as that of the 'I' itself—remains alien to *science as a profession*. They might interest the individual scientist, in the same way that the single scientist can believe in the Trinity, but upon it, science, *as science*, must *remain silent*, and the 'fact that science cannot give us this answer is absolutely indisputable'.[12] It is *responsible*, that is, capable only of answering sensibly formulated questions regarding the knowledges and operations that expand the power of human reason over nature in the immense area of the *Vernunftlose*. It would constitute the most illogical of leaps to another genre to maintain that, on the strength of such a power, it would be possible even to simply initiate a System of Freedom.

---

11 This sharply distinguishes Weber's Nietzsche from every other image of him of the period. I have repeatedly highlighted (although this has been largely ignored) this affinity, which moreover Weber declares explicitly, from *Krisis: Saggio sulla crisi del pensiero negativo da Nietzsche a Wittgenstein* (Milan: Feltrinelli, 1976) and *Pensiero negativo e razionalizzazione* (Venice: Marsilio, 1977), up to my introduction to Weber's *La scienza come professione: La politica come professione* (Milan: Mondadori, 2006).

12 Weber, 'Science as a Vocation', p. 17.

The scientist who affirmed it would *ipso facto* become *ir-responsible*. Even the social scientist? Certainly, she too. She can 'simply' compare different world views, different ethical systems, demonstrate their presuppositions and historical efficacy to the point of being able to point out, in entirely probabilistic terms, the consequences that can be derived from them. But never could she, as a scientist, establish their *value* on the basis of universal ends, ordering them hierarchically in light of salvation or the Good. 'Values' remain outside the scientific purview, both in the field of physical-mathematical sciences and in those of the so-called human sciences.

Hence, two *completely heterogeneous* sets of problems are foregrounded by Weber: on the one hand, establishing states of affairs, *Tatsachen*, and the effective relations between them, *Sachverhalte*, both in properly mathematical terms of the science of nature and in those logical-analytical ones proper to cultural-spiritual phenomena.[13] On the other hand, to pose the question around *value*, the question of how one *ought* to act, which seems to lead to the definition of the *friend and enemy* or, in any case, inevitably to that of *conflict*.[14] The field that such

---

13 The reference to Wittgensteinian language is entirely intentional. In the same way that Weber disenchants the liberatory powers of the scientific project, so Wittgenstein disenchants those of logic whenever it presumes to rationalize the forms of life (there is nothing more illogical or 'enchanted' than to expect man to be able to do without convictions or faiths, substituting for them logical notions). Even the distinction between the sphere of being and that of value, which lies at the heart of Emil Lask's thought, should be noted here. Disenchantment and political realism always go hand in hand—and demand a coherent logical formulation. See Agostino Carrino, *L'irrazionale nel concetto*: *Comunità e diritto in Emil Lask* (Naples: Edizioni scientifiche italiane, 1983). (Carrino also edited the Italian edition of Lask's *Rechtsphilosophie*). On Lask's thought, see the substantial monograph by Felice Masi, *Emil Lask*: *Il pathos della forma* (Macerata: Quodlibet, 2010).

14 How much Schmitt owes to the Weberian lesson is immediately evident—as in the restatement that no *Duty-Sollen* will ever be able to transform itself into *political* power and, hence, be able to truly act within a conflict ignoring the entire context produced by the process of rationalization-secularization. See part three of Julien Freund, *La crisi dello Stato tra decisione e norma* (Agostino Carrino ed.) (Naples: Leviathan, 2008).

a question throws open goes well beyond the problem of the function and general character of prophecy and demagogic charisma (prophecy and demagogy should, moreover, be considered to be polar opposites), opening precisely onto that of *politics as profession*. It is around this core element that Weber's perspective is concentrated. Hence, the opposition between two orders, the professional-scientific, on the one hand, and that of values, on the other, which might have seemed generic, configures and determines itself as a conflict between *scientific intellectual labour* and *political intellectual labour*. It is this conflict, the *inseparable distinction* between these two powers, that seems to Weber to mark the destiny of the epoch. It is the *rationalization* of this conflict that he attempts to assay.

How can one precisely define the nature of their *con*-flicting? We must first seek to clarify their logical path, Weber's *method*. In Weber, *Entwertung* (the process by which one projects, *Ent-wurf*, and accomplishes the distinguishing between scientific-rational analysis and prospecting of *values*) in no way assumes the meaning of general *absence of presuppositions*. Neither does he intend to 'prophesize' upon a *de-sacralizing* of all forms of vital experience (although he studies the phenomena that reveal the general tendency). We have seen that the presupposition of the *scientiam facere* is so fundamental as to coincide with the very principles of the form of rationality that dominates Western civilization and from which alone the intellectualization of contemporary life could be generated. *Entwertung* means only that no path can lead to such a presupposition and from these principles establish a scale of hierarchically ordered values between civilizations and world views. It is necessary to *renounce* (a keyword of the Goethian inheritance, dramatically lived by Nietzsche) the Western conception of philosophy-science, of *episteme*, as universal End. His *Beruf* in no way constitutes a *mission* of salvation for the life of the entire species.[15]

15 Husserl speaks in these terms in his 'magisterial' lessons on Fichte of 1917, in the afterword to *Ideen* of 1930 and again in *Krisis*. There is nothing more instructive than comparing these final pages of 'heroic' idealism to those of Weber, especially

This is the critical point. Can a presupposition 'renounce' asserting itself as a 'value' as well? Is it realistic to think such a thing? Can a presupposition constitute simply the foundation of a logical path defined in itself? Can it produce specific consequences within its specific area, without at the same time *asserting itself* [*farsi valere*] universally? Weber's analysis grounds itself in a purportedly logical distinction between the assumption of a presupposition and a *choice* of value. The presupposition is supposed to operate as a mere *hypothesis*, forming the basis for the production of arguments and conclusions. However, this distinction escapes all empirical and historical determination. That is, it can only be conceived of as a formal possibility. In concrete reality, the affirming of the value of the presupposition is always implicit in the act of presupposing. More than this: there is a firm *will* to assert the value of the presupposition by opposing it to the others. Every position, moreover, implies, or rather constitutes in itself an *op-position*. And the non-I that stands in opposition to the 'I' must necessarily be understood to be reconcilable with the 'I'. The 'I' *must* reconcile it to itself.[16] This *duty* necessarily resounds in the presupposition of *scientiam facere* that governs the modern West. The two spheres, being and duty, end up conflicting in reality. This would not happen, perhaps, if the method of science in Fichte's sense led, *according to its very principles*, to the Kingdom of Freedom. Is this an illusion? Weber states that it is. It is certainly the case that, historically, the presupposition of *scientiam facere* is determined in opposition to others; that is, it has acted as a *value* and a universally valid Value. Its extraordinary energy manifested itself as *at once* a will to knowledge and a will to domination. Disquiet in itself and *violence*

---

bearing mind that precisely in *Krisis*, Husserl ended up asking himself whether 'conceiving the world as the teleological product of the "I" ' was in truth nothing but a mere historical-factual *folly*. [I have translated the Husserl quotation from the Italian, as I have been unable to find the passage in English editions of Husserl's *The Crisis of European Sciences and Transcendental Phenomenology*— Trans.]

16 The centrality of the theme of the *Sollen* probably constitutes the Kantian trait of Fichte, upon which Hegel will insist—and, perhaps, this is what allows Fichte to be distinguished more clearly from Gentile's actualism.

towards the other. Never at peace in itself and never able to 'leave in peace' the other. Everything has been overwhelmed in that vortex that, in its promethean age, was called 'progress' (the 'great calamity of the faith in progress', as Burckhardt would have it). At the end of Hegel's *Phenomenology*, this destiny had already found its highest and in many ways definitive philosophical expression.

The scientist—exclusively focused on his own *Sache*, 'elected' by it—can think (or delude himself?) that all 'illusions are banned' from his own camp (but how, as Nicolai Hartmann adds, if his *operari* can never separate itself from 'both the private and historical flux of life'?).[17] However, the scientist can never, whether consciously or not, whether she forgets it or not, free herself from the presupposition, the veritable *archè* of her labour. Analogously, she will never be abstractly 'free' in the concrete exercise of her profession: the more the specialisms develop their own power, the more they must integrate in a social and political whole that orders from above [*sovra-ordinato*] the exercise of each. And so, Weber's disenchantment is also directed towards the fundamental early modern idea of *libertas philosophandi*. In the epoch of the full maturity of the process of rationalization, no scientific endeavour can be conceived as abstractly 'autonomous'. It is effective—and hence will be what it *ought* to be—only as part of a *system*. The *professions* form a single framework of functional dependencies. Contemporary productive Labour, the labour that determines the progress of truly *powerful* knowledge, can only be that of the *social brain*.[18] This *global* organization,

---

17 Hartmann's *Das Problem des geistigen Seins* (The Problem of Spiritual Being), the first edition of which was published in the fateful year 1933 (like Werner Jaeger's *Paideia*), can be rightly understood as a last-ditch attempt to affirm, with philosophical rigour, the civilizing mission of theoretical knowledge in all areas of the spirit, 'free' from the influence of *doxa*, that is, of 'public opinion'.

18 Weber cannot have read Marx's *Grundrisse*. And yet, the idea of a universal (Jungerian and Heideggerian) *Machenschaft* (machination) able to clasp in a unity the very *division* of labour, capable of turning its systematic division into a single power that which unites it as a whole, appears to me to be implicit in the whole framework of his analyses. Nothing can be understood of the successive discourses around Technology (in Heidegger as well) if one does not set out from such analyses.

which no single profession, nor their simple cooperation, could realize in themselves, is *politics* in its essence. This idea already exists in the original conception of the modern State. In many ways it represents the regulative idea that guides the latter's actions and that unfolds in all its power in the contemporary era. Rationalization *in politicis* means to project and construct the indispensable conditions for the highest point of development of the *augmentum scientiarum*.[19] Such *augmentum* would, in turn, be unable to succeed without being fostered and sustained by a political Order, that is, without constituting a fundamental factor of the latter's *project*. Concentrated, as she *ought* to be, on her specific profession, the scientist *does not* consider either the historical-cultural presuppositions of her work [*operare*] (that is, she does not *think* the foundations, the *archè* of her actions) or the problematic link with the dimension of value, or the dependency of her labour upon a political Order that appears to transcend her in the very moment in which she draws sustenance and near justification from it. We might go so far as to say that scientific labour supports itself precisely upon the *repression* of this order of problems, upon *not thinking them*: a repression of the foundations or the origin of the rationality that informs it, a repression of the effective power of its own ineliminable horizon of value, a repression of its own inevitable historical-political conditions. It goes without saying that the term 'repression' does not have a negative meaning: rather, it is precisely thanks to the 'value' of such repression, or perhaps more appropriately one might speak of such 'bracketing', that scientific labour is able to concentrate *on the thing* and to function and progress.

That means that the scientific point of view, disenchanted of all teleological illusion, must then still be *critiqued* within its limits, 'discovered' with respect to its un-said and its presuppositions and located realistically in its relations to the historical-political situation. In the contemporary world, there is no longer an abstract freedom of research conducted according to a regime of pure 'truth' that does not depend, as well, on choices at the level of political institutions, within priorities

---

19 See my essay 'Grandezza e tramonto dell'utopia' in Massimo Cacciari and Paolo Prodi, *Occidente senza utopie* (Bologna: Il Mulino, 2016).

established by the government of the State. However, this critical investigation does not rest upon science tout court, but on social sciences and philosophy. Were the sciences of nature to confront such problems, they would end up losing the necessary concentration, they would be unable to reclaim that island of the understanding of which Kant spoke by making it increasingly fertile and productive. It follows that no profession situated within the orbit of the process of rationalization and embraces the imperative of exactitude with ensuing forms of specialization, will be able to *decide* or to help decide within the polytheistic context of values. And no profession with valid instruments to affirm what ends should be pursued in the Civitas will ever arise. Nor will it possess any criterion to distinguish clearly the divine from the idolatrous. The sciences of culture, for their part, are only able to analyse that character that *values* assume and to determine (probabilistically, as we said) the consequences that derive from the transgression or obedience to them. Nevertheless, the process of rationalization will always tend to manifest as an *imperative*, based on the presuppositions that have been indicated, representing itself as a universal destiny or common destination. It will then be the duty of the social scientist, who is the legitimate heir of that process, to demonstrate how such presuppositions are *irrationalizable*, that is, are fruits of a *decision* that is itself unfounded. But nothing testifies with greater energy to the western form of rationality than the demonstration of the irrationality of every hierarchy of value. The scientist's *Wertfreiheit* will not, in short, ever be free from the value-being of its presupposition and its actual tendency (whether it affirms it or not) to *con-vince*,[20] of itself and for itself, other cultures and the entire Globe.

---

20 Cacciari plays on the word *convincere*, 'to convince', whose component elements are highlighted via hyphenation: *con-*, 'with', and *vincere*, 'to win': 'to conquer'. The suggestion is that the scientist advances the presupposition of 'value-free' science as the only legitimate, *valuable* way to proceed scientifically, which it spreads to other cultures, 'conquering' the entire globe. That is, that the 'value-free' nature of science is itself a (necessarily) scientifically unfounded value that is imposed. [Trans.]

Weber knows this well, and he is even more aware that the power of the technico-scientific apparatus could only fully express itself within a political Order and a social form of production that coheres with it. There is in him no space for the ideology of *Wertfreiheit*, no myth of the *Freigeist*. However, if one does not want to surrender to the siren call of reaction, on the one hand, or to the choir of revolution, on the other (that frequently proceed in a nefarious symbiosis), it is necessary to hold firm the ideal-typical distinction: the scientist must learn to remain silent over the drama of political decision or, if they are a social scientist, must limit themselves to the analysis of the nature of the gods in struggle; whereas the politician must enter the agon and must assume the role of a god against another god and be ready to endure all the consequences of their decision. It is a conflict between *acting consciousness* and *judging consciousness*, but no longer an ideally reconcilable one. For Hegel,[21] their fertile contradiction of one another—the judging consciousness wants its 'tatlosen Reden', its 'inept' chatter,[22] to be *reality*, and, for its part, the acting consciousness sees in 'discourse' nothing but the ineffectual and persists in its particularity—is achieved in reciprocal recognition, in 'das versöhnende Ja', in the Yes that reconciles them.[23] For Weber, however, conflict can compose itself only through the *renunciation* of both. The scientist renounces appearing as an essential factor of a System of Freedom; the politician renounces the possibility of grounding, 'precisely', the values and ends for which he fights upon rational foundations. It is the disenchantment of that synthesis of theory and praxis that informed the great idealist systems and their critics between 1830 and 1848, as well as that which an incautious Marxism will never cease to

---

21 See Georg Wilhelm Friedrich Hegel, 'Conscience; the Beautiful Soul, Evil, and Its Forgiveness' in *The Phenomenology of Spirit* (Terry Pinkard trans.) (Cambridge: Cambridge University Press, 2018), pp. 365–89.

22 Cacciari is perhaps alluding to the 'idle chatter' that appears in *The Phenomenology of Spirit*, p. 370 (but see also p. 373). However, the precise terms that Cacciari uses are neither those of the English nor of the most commonly used Italian edition of the *Phenomenology*. [Trans.]

23 Hegel, *Phenomenology of Spirit*, p. 389. [Trans.]

repeat. It is the radical disenchantment concerning the liberatory nature of scientific progress.

A critical and deconstructive genealogy, which has nothing to do with the polemic against the idea of profession to which we alluded to at the beginning. Those who, like Erik von Kahler,[24] opposed the Weberian *Beruf* conceived the process of professionalization or specialization of science as that which prevents the realization of a System of Freedom. From Weber's standpoint, this is simply absurd: the professions in no way prevent it, it simply has nothing to say on the matter. Not only does the return to a sort of 'first philosophy' capable of embracing and comprehending from their foundation the diverse forms of living experience express an impotent nostalgia in regard to the process of rationalization-specialization. Not only is the Vision that such a return calls for largely mythological or, in any case, bound to unsustainable metaphysical and theological presuppositions following the *crisis of foundations* that invested the entirety of European science at the end of the nineteenth century. Furthermore, such reactionary positions cannot see that what are perhaps the only spiritual values of this epoch are safeguarded by the specialist professions themselves, in their concentration, in their passion for exactitude, in the will for autonomy *despite it all.* They too, as we have seen, must be disenchanted, but this certainly cannot be done from the heights of the Magic Mountain of the Romantic and, what's more, in an unpolitical key.[25] Even less can this be done in name of a neo-humanist *Bildung* sustained by the myth of classical Greece.[26] The relationship between the forms of contemporary life and

---

24 See Erich von Kahler, *Die Krisis in der Wissenschaft* (1919). Ernst Troeltsch replied to Kahler through a broad consideration of the cultural climate that underpins the entire debate that followed Weber's conference, *Die Revolution in der Wissenschaft. Eine Besprechung von Erich von Kahlers Schrift gegen Max Weber* (1921).

25 A 'brilliant' misunderstanding, since it produces Mann's *Reflections of a Nonpolitical Man*, which are aimed fully at dividing, *deciding* the Romantic from liberalism.

intellect, its vital energy [*vita nervosa*], is irrevocable.[27] However, it is configured radically differently in the dimension of scientific intellectual labour as compared to the political one. Precisely this difference, which confers on the image of the epoch its character of radical *insecuritas*, also renders impossible the naively pessimistic affirmation that the configuration of such an image corresponds to the pure crumbling of the foundations of a spiritual life.

Alexander Schwab's position differs from that of von Kahler.[28] While he too defines the professions as a 'ruinous monster' that suck all energies, Schwab cultivates the idea that they might be 'educated', that is, that it might be possible to practice them while preventing them from ascending to Value. This is an idea that in different ways traverses all the *Kultur* of the epoch, even many representatives that are closer to technical-economic *action*. Yes, it is necessary *to form* a *professionalized* ruling class, but one that is free of the idolatry of specialisms. In other words, one that is able, on the back of the strength of spiritual *Bildung*, to maintain a critical distance, to not identify with the exercise of the specialist *Beruf*. The power that such a class is called upon to exercise must be legitimated by the superior spirituality that it is able to express, or that power will end up dissolving. This is the 'great bourgeois' idea to which we will need to return, of the possible 'reconciling Yes' of *Kultur*, and of technico-economic and political power, which draws distantly on the inspi-

---

26 This is the great philological tradition of *Humanismus*, from August Boeckh and Wilamowitz, to—with notable differences—Jaeger's *Paideia*. The historico-philological ideas of *Humanismus* perform a decisive function in the German politico-cultural climate straddling the world war. See Ulrich von Wilamowitz-Moellendorff, *Cultura classica e crisi tedesca* (Luciano Canfora ed.) (Bari: De Donato, 1977), which contains an anthology of political writings by Wilamowitz. I also touch on this in my *La mente inquieta: Saggio sull'Umanesimo* (Turin: Einaudi, 2019).

27 We find an analogous position in Georg Simmel, whose influence on Weber's *Weltanschauung* deserves particular attention. See also my introduction to Simmel's *Diario postumo* (Turin: Aragno, 2011).

28 Alexander Schwab, 'Beruf und Jugend', *Die weißen Blätter* 4(5) (May 1917).

ration of the mature Goethe and that we find again, differently declined, in Thomas Mann, in Walter Rathenau and even in Benedetto Croce.[29]

---

29 It is significant that Mann still feels close to Erich von Kahler in 1945, dedicating to him an affectionate encomium for his sixtieth birthday: 'His being, penetrated the looming uncertain menace of German tragedy. He became, to my mind, the most expert and painfully comprehending contemporary analyst of the German character and destiny.' Translated from the Italian in *Scritti minori*, Tutte le opere di Thomas Mann, VOL. 12 (Lavinia Mazzucchetti ed.) (Milan: Mondadori, 1958). Carl Schmitt had already heavily mocked these positions of the great writer. On Rathenau, see my *Walter Rathenau e il suo ambiente* (Bari: De Donato, 1979). The relationship between Mann and Croce is well-documented in *Carteggio 1930–1936* (Naples: Tolmino, 1999) (first published in *Archivio storico ticinese* 61 [1975]). However interesting it is, it fails to shed much light upon *the* question, which is to say, how Croce interpreted the catastrophe that had taken place (what Mann calls a 'murky *Zwischenfall*'), and how, conversely, Mann understood his own *Selbstüberwindung* in comparison to the ideas in his *Reflections*. To measure the difference between these bourgeois 'writ large', it is enough to consider that Mann writes to Croce of having been prepared for his self-overcoming 'by a great, lived educational experience: familiarity with the life and thought of Nietzsche', the author whose epochal importance Croce will continue to remain oblivious of, believing him perhaps, as a good Mediterranean [*latino*], to be an element of that 'impenetrable woodland' of German Romanticism of which Hofmannsthal spoke in his speech of 1927, 'The Written Word as the Spiritual Space of the Nation' (in *Hugo von Hofmannsthal and the Austrian Idea: Selected Essays and Addresses 1906–1927* [David S. Luft ed. and trans.] [West Lafayette, IN: Purdue University Press, 2011]). See Edoardo Massimilla, 'Benedetto Croce a Max Weber', *Archivio di storia della cultura* 29 (2016). On this question, see Biagio De Giovanni, *Libertà e vitalità: Benedetto Croce e la crisi della coscienza europea* (Bologna: Il Mulino, 2018). One should also note that the term 'bourgeois' should be used with great caution in relation to Croce, who attempted to critique it in an essay contained in *Etica e politica* (1931), 'Di un equivoco concetto storico: la "borghesia"', believing it to be vitiated by its instrumental reactionary or socialist uses, and considering it legitimate only in the economic dimension. The criticism is valid for all generalization but certainly not when the concept is specified in concrete historical analyses, as with Eric Hobsbawm's *The Age of Capital 1848–1875* (London: Abacus, 1988) [tellingly, the Italian edition is translated as *Il trionfo della borghesia* (The triumph of the bourgeoisie)—Trans.]. It counts even less if one understands by it, as Croce would like, that *homo oeconomicus* 'cannot have a spiritual

For that bourgeois who is perfectly disenchanted regarding the destiny of his class, that is, Max Weber, to be tardy in searching for a mediation between *Kultur* and *Zivilization* is not so much *improbus* so much as *vanus labor*.[30] For him, neither the one nor the other of the terms of

---

history'. Weber had explained how profound and active in the Economic itself is the action of *spirit*. Here, Croce's logic of the distinct is unable to arrive at or comprehend the whole of the *actual* (*die Wirkliche*).

[Croce introduced a modification to Hegel's dialectic, supplementing the dialectic of opposition/contradiction with a 'logic of the conceptual'. Very summarily, Croce criticized Hegel for extending to the fundamental regions of Spirit his logic of opposition, the dialectic of *aufheben*, where conceptual oppositions are not resolved in favour of one side or the other but in a higher category or moment that both negates and raises up the negatively opposed terms. Croce provides four such fundamental regions, which he extracts from Hegel, albeit with a certain interpretive violence: art, logic (philosophy), economics and ethics. Whereas in Croce's Hegel the various regions of Spirit are related dialectically—so, for example, philosophy is a form that resolves art within itself, negating the categories of the former and raising them up into philosophy which represents art's overcoming—for Croce each of these regions is *distinct*, possessing its own set of categories that other *distinct* regions of Spirit cannot intervene into. Hence the 'logic of the distinct'. The picture is rendered more complex still in that each distinct region remains that of a single Spirit. So, each region is both distinct but presupposed by the subsequent region, which in turn forms the presupposition of later regions, without a final culmination but rather in cyclical fashion, each rotation enriching by degrees the presupposed and the presupposing regions—Trans.]

30 Carl Schmitt, who in the years straddling the Great War was also profoundly influenced by the apocalyptic *Weltanschauungen* of the process of mechanistic uprooting that dominates the contemporary world, shared Weber's radically critical standpoint on all attempts to harmonize *Kultur* and capitalism (see the extraordinary interest for the poet Theodor Däubler and for the artistic-esoteric circles of Munich: Stefan Nienhaus, 'Carl Schmitt fra i poeti letterati' in Carl Schmitt, *Aurora boreale: Tre studi sugli elementi, lo spirito e l'attualità dell'opera di Theodor Däubler* (Naples: Edizioni scientifiche Italiane, 1995) [The Italian translation of Schmitt's *Theodor Däublers 'Nordlicht': Drei Studien über die Elemente, den Geist und die Aktualität des Werkes* (Munich: Müller, 1916)—Trans.]; see also Giuseppe Bevilacqua, *Letteratura e società nel secondo Reich* (Milan: Longanesi, 1977). Schmitt's assessments of Mann remained contemptuous till the last, and his satire on the figure of Rathenau

the apparent dilemma express the *Sache* or represent the reality of contemporary social relations. Life and intellect have been bound together, *con-fused* forever in the exercise of the professions. To separate them is pure nominalism. Arthur Salz grasped Weber's point of view when he affirmed that the age of insecurity could be confronted with courage only on the basis of principles of rational thought, but he moved away from it immediately and profoundly when he placed in strict analogy the power of scientific thought and that of political practice, which he considered to be natural allies in the establishment of Order.[31] In other words, Salz fully and uncritically assumed the presupposition of the political *value* of science as profession as well, whereas the dramatic centre of Weber's critique concerned precisely such a *value* and the ends that might be linked to them. With great ingenuity, even today widely shared, Salz was thereby able to speak of existence as a sort of accord between science and life, of an irenic conciliation between scientific rationality and the polytheism of values, which eliminated the conflict and 'rationalized' the necessity of decision that constitutes the essential dimension of the Political. A truly disenchanted knowledge, able to weigh, to calculate, to recognize its own finitude, does not limit itself to deterministically affirming the destiny of rationalization. Moreover, it is conscious that rationalization itself, setting out from rational presuppositions that cannot be founded, 'hides' *within itself* the conflict with the value dimension, and this constitutes its character. Realistically, the

---

contained in his early *Schattenrisse* (*Silhouettes*) from 1913 most certainly inspired the unforgettable character of Arnheim in Musil's novel. More generally, one should also insist upon the distance separating von Kahler and other Weberian critics from the most significant exponents of the Konservative Revolution, such as Hans Freyer and Arthur Moeller van den Bruck, whose analyses of the contradictions of the *Gestell* and geo-political vision are of a very different stature.

31 Arthur Salz, *Für die Wissenschaft: gegen die Gebildeten unter ihren Verächtern* (Munich: Drei Masken, 1921). We owe to Edoardo Massimilla some of the most important historiographic contributions, not only in Italy, to the study of this period and of the debate around Weber's essays. See his *Scienza, professione, gioventù: Rifrazioni weberiane* (Catanzaro: Rubbettino, 2008) and *Presupposti e percorsi del comprendere esplicativo: Max Weber e i suoi interlocutori* (Naples: Liguori, 2014).

process of rationalization thus affirms itself in a world in which the other forms of labour, while being *intellectual*, appear irreducible to that proper to *scientiam facere*. Amongst them, political praxis, *the Political*, is called upon to play a decisive part.

If science as a profession must, in the concrete unfolding of its exercise, renounce taking direct and active part in the *polemos* of values, it nevertheless belongs to the world, to the life of which it was said, at civilization's origins, that Polemos is the 'father'. The forms of organization and institutions of knowledge depend upon the whole order of the Political. The synapses of those institutions of knowledge and the social form of production will need to be powerfully influenced by the Political. Lastly, the very polemic against the professions in the name of the idea of *Kultur* must assume political significance: the idea of *Kultur* first establishes itself in polemical terms against *politics as a profession*, a profession consubstantial with the eruption of the organized masses on the scene of history and with the affirmation of modern democracy. Reaction and revolutionism become confused on this terrain: the two mass tendencies which cooperate in their conflict in the destruction of bourgeois democracy see in the professions nothing but a mechanical form of Duty. Both extol the unstoppable energy of the *movement* of life *versus* the form of organization. They both crave a *Deus adveniens* that only in the struggle against *Zivilization* can be presaged *per speculum*.[32] In contrast, all our reflections so far force us to grasp *the* problem of Weber, not so much in relation to the differences between scientific labour and political labour, so much as in that of the representation of the drama in which both necessarily participate as at once protagonists and antagonists.

---

32 It is the aura that pervades Benjamin's early writing, which Giorgio Agamben has rightly gathered under the title of one of them, 'Metafisica della gioventù' (*Metafisica della gioventù: Scritti 1910–1918* [Giorgio Agamben ed.], Opere di Water Benjamin, VOL. 1 [Turin: Einaudi, 1982]), a period that we can consider to end with *Zur Kritik der Gewalt* of 1921, where the violence of the law over life (a radical reconsideration of 'professional alienation') is opposed to revolutionary violence, which liberates life. In these years, Bloch too revisits the themes typical of the discussions of the period around the *geistige Arbeit*.

It will also be impossible to stop at the abstract opposition between responsibility in relation to the scientist's object of investigation and the practico-political form of the responsibility of the politician in relation to the *community of the 'I's*. The scientist also participates in the latter. And how then could he not have a precise and concrete *inter-est*[33] in the forms through which it evolves? The awareness of her own activity leads the scientist to confront the complexity of life in which she works and that to an extraordinary extent determines her. The political dimension constitutes the immanent aporia of science as a profession. The latter would never be reduced to a private dimension (the popular adage: the scientist is free to take part in the life of the community according to his 'pleasure'), in the same way that, entirely unrealistically, a certain lay thinking reduces religious denomination, the conviction of 'faith', to a 'matter of the heart'. A similar 'logic of the distinct' contradicts *radicitus* the complexity and contemporary interweaving of 'social circles'; it deludes itself into dialogically resolving the conflict of values, and it removes the knot of will and power that is the foundation of the very process of the rationalization and disenchantment of the world.

---

33 Cacciari's neologism *inter-esse* associates togetherness, interrelation (*inter*) with 'being', the root of *essere*, 'to be'. *Interesse* also means 'interest'. This is relatively straightforward to render in English as I have with 'inter-est', where again *inter* is a relational prefix, whereas *est* comes from the French 'to be', drawing on the Anglo-Norman—ultimately Latinate rooted—*interesse*. The Heideggerian *Mit-sein*, alluded to here, is rendered in English translations as 'Being-with'. [Trans.]

III

NEW CENTAURS

There is no conflict of values that does not involve a *decision* over the social and political Order produced from such a conflict. The conflict of values always assumes a *constituent* form. Indeed, whoever participates in it acts with the aim of resolving it. And so, *who* will decide? It will not be science, as we have seen, and yet the question remains fundamental for science as well. Will the Political decide? Even in Weber, the affirmative answer seems obvious. But which Political? That which could take shape on the basis of a simple logic of the distinct, the Political of the liberal Order? Certainly not. All our reflections so far lead us to deny it. Only a Political that 'internalizes' the destiny of rationalization, then, a Political able to posit itself as *analogous* to scientific intellectual labour. Without a competent technical-bureaucratic apparatus, without organization, without competencies, the Political is not a *profession* and so will necessarily end up being ineffective to govern a world dominated by technical-scientific powers. The Political that does not want to or does not know how to professionally structure itself and, at the same time, to endow itself with powerful administrative and bureaucratic structures is a case of mere will to *impotence*. Holding firm, *Festhaltung*, the general interest of the state, requires a class of executive employees that cannot conceive their performances to be merely incidental, discretionary or arbitrary. *Public service* demands 'those who perform it to sacrifice [*Aufopferung*] the independent and discretionary satisfaction of their subjective ends, and thereby gives them the right to find their satisfaction in the performance of their duties, and in this alone.'[1] This high liberal-bourgeois conception of bureaucracy is presupposed by

1 Hegel, *Elements of a Philosophy of Right*, §294, p. 333; but see also §§289–96.

Weber as a regulative idea. But in its turn, this conception is made to depend upon the formative process: impartiality, probity, scrupulous observance of the law, kindness and so the essential attributes of the 'true' bureaucrat can only be the product of a *Bildung* of the customs of thought (*sittliche und Gedankenbildung*). The Political is itself called upon to form a competent bureaucratic *caste* capable also of 'resisting' the changes of government and the inevitable ensuing legislative occasionalisms.

What would occur if the Politician were to take on the traits of prophecy or of pure demagogy (characteristics to be clearly distinguished on the ideal-typical plane, but that are continually combined in historical experience)? He might pretend to shackle the necessary *libertas philosophandi* of the scientist to his own ends, desires, or utopias, thereby preventing or blocking the scientist's productive energy. And were the values of the Political to conflict with the *augmentum scientiarum*, one would, in the end, in the contemporary world, arrive at the suicide of the Political itself. Because today it is the *value* that technical-productive progress assumes and the increase in wealth production that it essentially comports, that constitutes the foundation of political Auctoritas itself. Here lies the paradox: it is precisely the *Wertfreiheit* of the scientific profession that will result in the constitution of the *value* against which to measure the real efficacy of political praxis. In the meantime, the Political will remain a profession, that is, *intellectual labour*, insofar as it can orient itself in accordance with the paradigm of technical-scientific endeavour. Were we to follow such a view to its ultimate consequences, however, we would have to conclude that the true professional politician, fully aware of the destiny of the disenchantment of the world, will be the one who adopts as his *duty* the rationalization of all the areas of life in accordance with the form of scientific rationality. That is, it will be the one who works for the progressive disappearance of their profession's *autonomous* character.

This result of the *neutralization* of the Political is, however, impossible, because the mere attempt to pursue it is already an eminently *political* act.[2] The neutralization of the autonomy of the Political is *politics* to the highest degree. The assertion of the non-value or even *dis-value* of the Political belongs entirely to the conflict of values that is represented on the scene of the Political itself. We shall return to this decisive aspect in the conclusion. For now, limiting ourselves to following Weber's reasoning, it is plain that if the difference between the two fundamental forms of intellectual labour were to take antinomic forms, if the decision of the one were essentially 'located in nothing', *à la* Stirner (an author very present in Schmitt, incidentally),[3] and the responsibility of the other exclusively and abstractly concerned its own *Sache* without any other *con*-science of the forms of life, 'communication' between them would be forbidden—and an Order, in this ontologically *in-secure* epoch, would become an unreal possibility. Even less realistic is the idea of a mediation established between them and guaranteed by a third power. There are no tribunals to adjudicate such conflicts. And no longer does Dike descend from Olympus, sent by Zeus, to steer the judges of our Areopagi. For an Order to be conceivable, it is necessary that science and politics, inasmuch as both are professions, each find within themselves the factor that renders them mediatable. The extraordinary straining of Weber's discourse aims at this: to identify the field upon which the powers of the

2 Carl Schmitt, 'The Age of Neutralizations and Depoliticizations', *Telos* 96 (1993): 130–142. In his studies, Gianfranco Miglio has focused on the idea of neutralization in 'divergent accord' with Schmitt (see volume two of *Le regolarità della politica* [Milan: Giuffré, 1987]).

3 'I have known Max Stirner since *Unterprima* [the eighth year of German secondary school]. [. . .] What explodes today was prepared before 1848. The fire that burns today was laid at that time. There are certain uranium mines in the history of the spirit [. . .]. Poor Max definitely belongs here.' Carl Schmitt, *Ex Captivitate Salus* (Matthew Hannah trans.) (Cambridge: Polity Press, 2017), pp. 64–65. It should be noted that the process of specialization involves, for each 'specialist' *as well*, a radical awareness of their *autonomy*, of their being unable to 'assure' themselves of anything but the efficacy of that form of doing for which they feel a vocation. In such a way, even the representative of what for Mann was the quintessentially 'great bourgeois' spirit, Goethe, could appear to some interlocuters to be 'founded on nothing'.

epoch can *encounter one another in their clashing* [*scontrandosi incontrarsi*]; that are able to render their very conflict productive, recognizing it and transforming it into a factor not only of development but of *democratization*;[4] and this field appears to be only identifiable with that of the concept of *responsibility*.[5] For the Politician, however, it is a case of a *global responsibility*, so to speak: the Politician is not only called upon to *respond*, to be held accountable for all the consequences of her projects and actions and for the means through which she intends to pursue her ends. As a profession, the Politician is called upon, on the one hand, to calculate, measure, to analyse by analogy with the method of scientific labour but, inasmuch as she is, on the other hand, explicitly a participant in the struggle on the terrain of values, she will be responsible for her choices and, hence, for the non-rationalizable basis involved in her decisions. The global responsibility of the Politician is to know how to *give a reason* for one's actions and, at the same time, to acknowl-

4 That is, never give up wanting to translate Polemos with relationship-relation-measure-*logos*: this is also the 'measure taken' [*linea di condotta*] by the political Weber, testified to by all his contributions on the constitution of the Republic and, in particular, in *Parlament und Regierung in neugeordneten Deutschland* (1918), which Croce had wanted to have immediately translated (the Italian edition by Enrico Ruta (1919); a new Italian translation was published in 1982 by Laterza with an important introduction by Francesco Fusillo). There is no 'passion' for democracy, but he thought that, in the present conditions, it was the only way to form responsible political leadership. [*Linea di Condotta* is the Italian translation of Brecht's *Die Maßnahme*, sometimes translated in English as *The Measures Taken* or *The Decision*. The Italian translation of the Brecht is also used as the title of the introduction to Mario Tronti's seminal *Operai e capitale* (Workers and Capital), and literally means 'course of action'. Cacciari may well be alluding to the Brecht and, possibly, the Weber-inspired Tronti text as well—Trans.]

5 One can find an analogous *pathos* of responsibility in the mission that Husserl entrusts to philosophy. Duty and responsibility form the key terms of the *Bildungsbürgertum*, but in Weber they are declined in a decisively practical way, capable of forever barring the road of any *unpolitical* reaction. Notwithstanding the differences that we have observed, this is true also for Mann, for Cassirer and for Croce.

edge oneself as *guilty* of the insurmountable irrational component expressed in this very acting. Such a component is absolutely not foreign to the presuppositions of science; and yet, the scientist in his concrete *operari* can ignore it or bracket it, that is, appear to not be responsible for it—an attitude that is impossible for the Politician, whose essence consists in knowing how to decide, thereby determining the *state of exception* itself. Science helps to predict, but not to make decisions. It is, in any case, on the basis of the concept of responsibility, and only to the extent that it is adopted as the effective value of acting, that intellectual labour and political labour can think to find an effective mediation. The concept of responsibility constitutes the slender strip of land along which science and politics, knowledge and power are able to meet; the *yardstick* that enables them to be *com-pared.*[6] Naturally, it is a case of a politics *and of a science* united in the ability to discern the truth of facts, distinguishing being from what ought-to-be, and that have both renounced all pretensions to salvation, all prospects of happiness,[7] as well as any theological-eschatological connotations. If the daemon of politics is the absolute antithesis to the god of love ('The [. . .] demon [. . .] of politics lives in an intimate and reciprocal contrast with the God of love as well as with the Christian God as institutionalized in the Christian churches, and it is a tension that can erupt at any time into an insoluble

---

6 Cacciari takes the Italian for 'compare', *commisurare*, and inserts a hyphen *com-misurare*, to emphasize two component elements of the word. From the Latin prefix *com-*, which means 'with', 'together', and the word *misurare*, 'to measure'. This is strictly untranslatable, although 'compare' comprises the same prefix and the Latin *par*, meaning equal, which is at least a term of measure. [Trans.]

7 The distance from the author of *Mitteleuropa*, Friedrich Naumann, is evidenced by the disenchantment from all types of teleologism (as from all philanthropic pacifism: see the article that well-summarizes Weber's *irdische Politik* (earthly politics): 'Zwischen zwei Gesetzen' in *Gesammelte politische Schriften* [Tübingen: Mohr / Siebeck, 1958]). See Ugo Gastaldi, 'Max Weber tra protestantismo e capitalismo' in *Protestantismo e capitalismo* (Turin: Claudiana, 1983). Weber will accuse Naumann of being *un-politisch* ('Zur Gründung einer National-Sozialen Partei' in *Gesammelte politische Schriften*).

conflict',[8] *doing politics*, as Machiavelli teaches us as well, always remains a *knowing* how to access evil, not merely so as to be its accomplice), science as a profession, according to its own delimitations, also ignorant of that god's *mandatum novum* (the 'true' scientist confesses his own *docta ignorantia* concerning it, while the one now sired to the 'spirit of capitalism' laughs at it for the benefit of the markets). Responsibility and disenchantment together form an inseparable ensemble for both.

On careful observation, the dissonant accord attempted by Weber between the two professions tends to 'save' the daemon of both, allowing one to see the novelty of their contemporary arrangements as a transformation of their traditional figures rather than as 'creations' ex novo. It is necessary to respond to the revolutionary intoxication, harbinger of the darkest reaction (so rings out the 'prophetic' final words of *Politik als Beruf*), through a historical reflection as well. Those old teachers who stepped forth nostalgically before the yearning for the *Novum* to flaunt their laboriously accumulated experience, loaded with delusions, will certainly have seemed detestable to Weber, as they did to the young Benjamin.[9] The impatience of the 'seekers' can never be 'disciplined' by a *Humanismus* 'in the service' of spiritual heirs,[10] nor by the seriousness with which one applies oneself to one's own specialism. However, as far as it is *scientifically* necessary to overcome one's delusions with respect to the efficacy of *docere* in orienting life's direction, it is equally necessary to demonstrate the ideological-mythological character of all ideas of radical renewal, of absolute *decision* from the past, of a redeeming futurity. Necessities that are not so much theoretical as practical-political,

---

8 Weber, 'Science as a Vocation', p. 90.

9 See Walter Benjamin, 'Die Jugend schwieg' in *Gesammelte Schriften*, VOL. 2, PART 1 (Rolf Tiedemann and H. Schweppenhäser eds) (Frankfurt am Main: Suhrkamp, 1972), pp. 66–67, first published in *Die Aktion* 3 42 (18 October 1913), coll. 979–81, under the pseudonym A(rdor).

10 See Hofmannsthal's beautiful lecture held in Munich in 1927, to which we have already referred: 'The Written Word as the Spiritual Space of the Nation' in *Hugo von Hofmannsthal and the Austrian Idea: Selected Essays and Addresses 1906–1927.*

since these ideas, however irrational, or perhaps precisely for this reason, can assume an immense efficacy and lead, through an inexorable heterogenesis of ends, to the darkest reaction. Hence, science as a profession is still the heir, in Weber, to that *dis-interested* character that cannot be unmoored from economic interests nor from religious and *political* questions, which can even be derived from ancient *theoria* (if it were not for the fact that this, as we have seen, depends upon metaphysical suppositions that are completely foreign to *scientiam facere*). Moreover, Weber grasps how the Politician can connect to scientific labour on the grounds of an ethics of responsibility, that is, can in the final instance only decide based on the force of his *convictions*. His *virtus* thus consists in being able to mediate the two dimensions. This is a precarious accord, at the very limits of impracticability. Certainly, a classic *phronesis* will not be sufficient to realize it. And yet, trying and trying again should characterize the politics of any true statesperson worthy of her epoch. ('In this sense an ethics of conviction and an ethics of responsibility are not absolute antitheses but are mutually complementary, and only when taken together do they constitute the authentic human being who is *capable* of having a "Beruf zur Politik."')[11] Thus, the *Beruf* for politics necessarily exceeds the order of the professions. But, for Weber, that *must* take place precisely in the sense of the *Aufhebung*, that is, of the re-positioning of the rational responsibility that characterizes the order of the profession on a different plane, which for him, in the end, is evidently also a higher plane.[12] Weber's problem is, once again, the modes of relation, of continuity, of possible 'dialogue' between forms of intellectual labour, not the logic by which these are distinguished. And it is *the* problem that characterizes the epoch of complete rationalization for him.

---

11 Weber, 'Science as a Vocation', p. 92.

12 In Weber, we hear the echo of a sort of primacy of *praxis* as an *architectonic techne* par excellence in an almost classic sense. A primacy that has the *duty* to affirm itself via all the conflicts and contradictions that we have pursued to this point and that in no way pretends to constitute itself as a *political philosophy* of universal value. The immense distance of Weber from the Strausses and Voegelins can be measured on this terrain.

In the context of the universal mobilization of social and intellectual forces, of mass organizations, the Politician 'exceeds' the dimension of the professions, but he must do so *professionally*, so to speak, if he does not want to be knocked out by the technical-scientific and economics powers of the epoch. In this epoch, could purely intellectual labour remain neutral towards the Political? Could its *Wertfreiheit* be understood to be mere dis-interest in *praxis*' domination? Not at all. It can only be a case of an *interested* autonomy. Moreover, we have already seen the historical-political and value determination of the principles that found it. We can now add that the scientific profession must acknowledge as its own *duty* (a very concrete *Sollen* born out of its own interests) the struggle against any Politician who overwhelms all ethics of responsibility with the *pathos* of mere conviction. For Weber, the point of view of science is therefore fundamental for the current characterization of the Political itself. What is the operation being attempted here? To *convince* the professions, *professional labour*, to the highest active and mindful *inter-esse* in the *victory* of *politics as a profession*, and so, in a responsible Politician on the model of responsibility and with the ethics of duty which have been historically incarnated in professional labour. Analogously, the Politician must be convinced that in the future she will be able to *count/possess-power* [*valere-potere*][13] only by adopting technico-bureaucratic traits, that is, to possess the capacity to measure and calculate, to be able to realistically analyse a situation, aspects that have already found their paradigm in the idea of *Beruf*.

---

13 *Valere-potere* literally means 'to have value' in the sense of 'to count', and 'to have power to', that is, 'to be capable of'. Hence the rather ungainly English translation, which thankfully need not reappear. [Trans.]

IV

DOUBLE DREAM

What does intellectual labour, profession, mean? Mitteleuropean *Kultur* at the turn of the century replied: the *bourgeoisie*. 'What would *Kultur* be if it were not bourgeois?' was repeated on all sides, faithfully believing that with this they were following Goethe's footsteps. Thomas Mann says it in an epigraph to his great book of 1918, *Reflections of a Nonpolitical Man*, and then repeats it in the essay from 1932, 'Goethe als Repräsentant des bürgerlichen Zeitalters'.[1] This is the unequivocal testimony of the continuity of his own spiritual world. In *Reflections*, the professional ethics that guarantees 'the dominance of order over mood, of the lasting over the momentary, of quiet work over genius' is carried out in a key that is as much a-political as much as *in politicos*.[2] Far more than a declaration of estrangement from or disinterest in the Political, *Reflections* represents a declaration of war against political praxis, inasmuch as it is intrinsically involved in the contemporary world's process of democratization, in its conservative as in its liberal and revolutionary currents. It is to such a *Kultur* that Weber's essays polemically respond. For Weber, it is necessary to think and project a Political capable of corresponding to the values of that ethics of duty that is imposed in

1 Thomas Mann, 'Goethe als Repräsentant des bürgerlichen Zeitalters', *Die Neue Rundschau* 4 (April 1932): 434–62. See Thomas Mann, 'Goethe as Representative of the Bourgeois Age' in *Essays of Three Decades* (Helen Tracy Lowe-Porter trans.) (New York: Vintage, 1957), pp. 66–92. [Trans.]

2 Cacciari fails to mention that here Mann is quoting from György Lukács' pre-Marxist work, *Soul and Form* (1911). See Thomas Mann, *Reflections of a Nonpolitical Man* (W. D. Morris et al. trans) (New York: New York Review of Books, 2021), p. 84. [Trans.]

professional labour, stripped of rhetoric and ideology. That is to say, it is necessary to realize a 'great bourgeois' *politics*. To this day, this has always been missing, and its absence has created our present. In Mann's self-overcoming, *Selbstüberwindung*, his lecture 'On the German Republic' of 1922,[3] he seems to adopt a similar perspective. But he has in no way substantially modified his idea of *Kultur* of 1918 and the intrinsic relationship that it has with bourgeois ethics. It is that same idea that he now proposes can assume a political character: the professions are called, in alliance with the Political, to form a world in the image of that *Bildung* to edify the life of the entire community in its own image. The bourgeois spirit no longer needs to 'contemplate' the state as, in Nietzsche's phrase, the 'coldest of all cold monsters', as an indifferent or hostile power, but rather *make it its own*. In Weberian terms: the bourgeoisie is called—to save itself too—to give rise to a responsible political class, one that is equal to the real situation that had sprung from the catastrophe of the War. To hold to the dissension between *Kultur* and the Political, however the latter is declined, would represent for the bourgeoisie the worst policy, that of impotence, and for Germany as a whole a surrender to demagogic-revolutionary forces. To educate *Bildung* and *Kultur*, that is, *the spirit of the bourgeoisie*, to the Political, to disenchant it to the point it comprehends the necessity of realizing *in politicis* the principles of its own ethics. This is the significance of Weber's writings on intellectual labour. However, in Weber, that was supposed to represent a *turning point*, not a passage, which could only oblige a radical *self-critique* of the idea of *Kultur* that had developed in the 'world of yesteryear'. It is precisely that 'leap' that imposes itself upon him, which the great author Thomas Mann would like to consider to be non-existent, or pursuable through a 'reasonable' bridge, running from the *Reflections* to the 1922 lecture 'On the German Republic'. Since Mann had himself debuted with the saga of *Buddenbrooks*, which represented the crisis of that world, this is an insuperable ambiguity.[4]

---

3 See Thomas Mann, 'On the German Republic' in *Reflections of a Nonpolitical Man*, pp. 507–47.

4 See Alberto Asor Rosa, *Thomas Mann o dell'ambiguità borghese* (Bari: De Donato, 1971). Reprinted in *Le armi della critica* (Turin: Einaudi, 2011). It is an ambiguity

If democracy turns out to be the scene of a conflict of values represented by demagogic politicians animated by irrational convictions and only 'responsible' in relation to the assertion of the latter, the distinction between ethics of the professions and politics will turn into an absolute separation. On the one hand, science 'concentrated' upon itself; on the other, the will to power of the Political prepared to decide without a knowledge of reality, without calculation of the consequences of its acting, forgetful of its own past. In short, without *measure*, *masslos*—that *measure* that for Mann characterizes the bourgeois age but that Nietzsche had already seen dissolve. At this point, Weber's idea of responsibility fully reveals the end that animates it: it demands of bourgeois ethics a reversal of its original perspective so as to become the protagonist of a democracy in which the community of 'I's supports itself on the recognition, on the mutual comprehension of the fundamental powers of intellectual labour and political labour. A democracy where power is held by those who understand the necessity of the *reciprocal responsibility* of such powers—moreover: of their active collaboration, their historic compromise, thereby becoming able to confront revolutionary energies, revolutionary *violence* from whatever side it comes. The bourgeois *code* must inform democratic institutions of itself, connecting parliamentarianism with *Humanismus*, and the idealist ethic with the principles of the rule of law.

Even Mann's path from the Unpolitical to the Political (or from that formidable delusion for the Political that marks the course of the German bourgeoisie from the 1848 revolution until the Great War) is

---

that in Mann is irresolvable: in his essays on Goethe, as in the one on Schopenhauer, he is able to ruthlessly grasp the end of the 'world of yesteryear', and yet concludes: 'The great sons of the bourgeoisie' have been able to ascend 'to a super-bourgeois spiritual dimension', demonstrating in this way that 'boundless possibilities lie in the bourgeois stage, possibilities of unlimited self-liberation and self-conquest' ('Goethe as Representative of the Bourgeois Age' in *Essays of Three Decades*, p. 91 [translation modified—Trans.]). For the Mann of the 1920s, the exponent of this possibility continued to be Nietzsche, as it was for Hofmannsthal. This was an immense error, for Nietzsche would have said anything but that he represented the self-overcoming of the *Bürgersinn*.

characterized by the passage to an idea of democracy able to *save* within itself, as its own soul, the 'great bourgeois' ethic. This is an idea we also find in Ernst Cassirer in his defence of the Republican Constitution.[5] Outside of politics, one cannot be 'men of culture', stated Mann in the lecture on Wagner with which he as yet unwittingly took leave of Germany: 'Sufferings and Greatness of Richard Wagner'.[6] However, he is unaware of what metamorphoses the pursuit of such as an aim must bring for both *political labour* and *intellectual labour*. For him, it is that ethic, as such, that it is necessary to conserve—and precisely its conservation implies the duty to *politicize it*. The bourgeois *Beruf*, the bourgeois *profession of faith* that is incarnated in the absolute seriousness of labour, must also learn to manifest itself as *political* will. Democracy permits it—preaches the great writer! The youth that protest before the *Selbstüberwindung*, that considered his present position a betrayal of the spirit of the *Reflections*, haven't understood it, they rather appear to refuse to understand it: Mann almost 'bellows' that nothing prevents democracy from becoming *the government of the best*, which is to say, of those who know how to interpret and mediate between the professions and politics. Cannot the greats of Romanticism be read in this way, he insists? Is Novalis so far from that bard of democracy, Walt Whitman, the *American* par excellence?[7] No destiny compels one to think that democratic politicization must assume the form of a quarrelsome parliamentarianism, unmeasured, irresponsible and plebeian.[8] Why should democratization necessarily result in the assertion of the spiritually

---

5 See Ernst Cassirer, 'The Idea of a Republican Constitution' (Seth Berk trans.), *The Philosophical Forum* 49 (2018): 3–17.

6 See Thomas Mann, 'Sufferings and Greatness of Richard Wagner' (1933) in *Essays of Three Decades*, pp. 307–53. [Trans.]

7 The lecture 'On the German Republic' is spasmodically engaged in clarifying and grounding such paradoxes, as if Mann could already see, long before his exile at the start of the Weimar period, the relationship with American democracy as the only way out of the European politico-cultural catastrophe.

8 Croce had already polemicized with the Mann of the *Reflections* in a book review at the time (now to be found in his *Carteggio*).

poorest mass movements?[9] But to realize the 'type' of democracy able to select the best, it is necessary for all the youth to commit themselves to it. A *furor politicus* is necessary, one that is as energetic as the philosophical and the artistic one that had characterized the great exponents of the bourgeois spirit, from Goethe through to Mann himself. In other words, the paradox of an *aristocratic democratization* pervades the entirety of Mann's thinking. This is by no means a merely literary paradox—it can be found, if one knows how to look beyond the bear words, also in Weber's disenchanted analysis, in the *ought-to-be* of a Politician who is able to *heroically* weld together in his person the ethics of responsibility and the ethics of conviction. The difference, and it is an essential one, lies in the fact that the 'new parliament and new government', which Weber reflects upon, only ever demands a 'relative' accord between *professions*, between specialized forms of *geistige Arbeit* that have traversed and completed the *improbus labor* of their radical disenchantment.

Mann's position, however, is not that of the conservative revolutionaries;[10] and even less is this true of Cassirer. While nationalist elements marked by the idea of an *organic community* can be found in it as they can in Mann, this current, despite the conspicuous inner differences,

---

9 See Georg Simmel, *Grundfragen der Soziologie* (1917). [Translated as *The Sociology of Georg Simmel* (K. H. Wolff ed. and trans.) (Glencoe, IL: The Free Press, 1950).] All these themes should be revisited in the light of Elias Canetti's *Crowds and Power* (1960).

10 On the 'Conservative Revolution' and on the breadth of the movements and positions that such a term seeks to encompass, there is a vast and extremely diverse set of contributions; a good place to start is Stefan Breuer, *Anatomie der Konservativen Revolution* (Darmstadt: Wissenschaftliche Buchgesellschaft, 1993) [See also Stefan Bruer, 'Between "Conservative Revolution", aesthetic fundamentalism and new nationalism: Thomas Mann's early political writings', *History of the Human Sciences* 11(2) (1998): 1–23—Trans.]. What separates it entirely from intellectuals such as Mann (despite the similarity of some of the authors' position, of their readings and more) is its sharp aversion towards the republican constitution. The fact remains that the osmoses of the idea of 'conservation' between openly reactionary and democratic 'openings' are continual in the milieu of the *Bildungsbürgertum*.

remained distinctly anti-democratic. For Mann, as for Weber, the contemporary Political situation cannot but be that of democracy—but here lies the either/or: either a democracy that is structured by the relation of professional responsibility to political responsibility, a relation that is not 'discutidora', but that is capable of leading to rational decisions; or a plebiscitary democracy, where the Leader and his court, the Party or the Movement, identify their *kratos* with popular sovereignty. Either a democracy whose soul remains that of 'great bourgeois' *Kultur*, aristocratically detached from the 'dull acceptance of the world and their profession'[11] in its very being-in-the-world, and remaining concentrated on its *Beruf*, or the democracy of massified, commanded, equivalent labour, out of whose compact mass emerges the sheer unfoundedness of political decision.

Weber and Mann only separate themselves from this perspective, as from that of a merely procedural democracy reduced to the expression of a vote, to the extent that they attribute to the democratic regime the possibility that it can assume *ethical* characteristics appropriate to the 'great bourgeois' age. In Weber, there is a full re-evaluation of the idea of profession and its application to political labour. In Mann, there is a rediscovery, in the highest expressions of *Kultur*, of the possible accord with the process of democratization. Where lies the difference between the supreme *orator*, the authentic reincarnation of the *vir bonus dicendi peritus*, of *Von deutscher Republik* and the author of *Politik als Beruf*? Certainly not in the difference between artist and scientist, between the artist who creates his own world, in which no 'progress' is possible, and the scientist, even a social one, who participates in a research community that is ever more organized and links its members in a single 'brain'. The real difference is between the faith in the Romantic, interpreted variously: on the one hand, faith in the Goethean inheritance dominated by 'tenacious hard work' and 'calm perseverance' (Mann), *which excludes the tragic principle* (and consequently venerates an image of Nietzsche that is almost subsumed in the figure of 'Goethe as Representative of the

---

11 Weber, 'Science as a Vocation', p. 93.

Bourgeois Age'), and, on the other hand, the radical disenchantment over the political effectiveness of such a tradition. The Romantic in Weber remains, ultimately, what it is for Schmitt: unpolitical nostalgia, mere *Streben* that imagines the overcoming of the necessity of state order and of its positive law. The aim of government, here, consists in rendering itself superfluous, affirmed Fichte, in *ending*, that is, it consists in overcoming its own finitude by 'opening itself' to the Kingdom of Freedom (and it is here that we can measure his distance from Hegel). Nietzsche, on the other hand, is the one who, for Weber too, demolishes the inheritance of the Novalis and Fichte. Nothing remains, then, but the ethics of the professions, although one entirely comprehended within the destiny of intellectualization and rationalization. Yes, the obtuse acceptance of the professions must be overcome, but it can only be so in the sense of the overcoming the unpolitical, in the sense of the commitment to the construction of the Republic. 'Great bourgeois' *Kultur* only sediments the sober thought of a mediation between productive intellectual labour and political praxis. Yet one must ask oneself, do sobriety and realism of thought here also form the foundation of a political project, that is, do they effectively *count* [*valgono*]? Or is it not rather a case of a 'double dream'? The dream of a *Bildungsbürgertum* that is capable of producing a political *culture*, on the one hand, and on the other, of a process of democratization able to select the best, the *aristoi*? To Walter Benjamin, this dream appears to have been definitively exhausted in 1932, when he presents along with Willy Haas a collection of citations of the 'great bourgeois', an anthology of the epoch when the bourgeoisie 'still spoke of things as they were' (*Vom Weltbürger zum Grossbürger*).

However, only according to the perspective of Weberian *realism* (that can even be distantly detected in the pages of the young Benjamin) can the question arise concerning the essential significance of such a 'double dream'. The coherence and rationality of the idea are insufficient to 'justify' it. It is necessary, rather, to demonstrate its concrete practicability. That is, it is necessary to *measure* the power of the subjects analysed so far and whether such power leads or can be mobilized towards the indicated ends. Do the professions and the bourgeoisie constitute a historical unity? Perhaps, but it's not enough. It is necessary to grasp in what form this 'alliance' is able to manifest itself today. Has political labour become professionalized? Perhaps—and certainly this goes in the direction of bourgeois spirit, contrasting with all forms of demagogic-plebiscitary democracy. But it is necessary to see what *power* the Political can exert on the system of 'free'-professions,[12] in terms of what today it represents, what it *counts* as. In terms of a philosophy of history 'writ large', the problem had already been posed by Fichte himself at the end of the *Goethezeit*:[13] how did the passage occur that led from the ethics of the *I ought*, from the rigorous intra-worldly asceticism that informs the Great Revolution itself, to the utilitarian empiricism of the 'commercial State', to the egoistic pursuit of ones' individual well-being? How could the *duty* to advance *Kultur* become transformed into the need for an uninterrupted satisfaction of the desires and needs of the 'private' subject? How could the System of Freedom be reduced to this? Which is to say, to 'accomplished sinfulness' (Fichte), which involves an adaptation to the world that loses all passion for Truth (philosophy) and for God (religion). What forces have broken the 'progress' passing from the System of Knowledge, *Wissenschaftslehre*, to the ethics,

---

12 *Professioni libere* is what we would more typically call the self-employed (those who provide a service for a fee). Literally this translates as 'free professions', which highlights the fact of not being directly, formally within a managerial, administrative or organizational hierarchy. Cacciari surrounds '*libere*' with scare quotes, suggesting that this freedom, today, is certainly problematic. There are cases of the use of 'free professions' in English; see, for example, Charles E. McClelland, 'The Organization of the "Free" Professions: Medicine, Law, Engineering, and Chemistry' in *The German Experience of Professionalization* (Cambridge: Cambridge University Press, 1991), pp. 73–97. [Trans.]

13 I am referring specifically to the lectures that compose the *Grundzüge des gegenwärtingen Zeitalters* (1804–1806). [Johann Gottlieb Fichte, *Characteristics of the Present Age* (William Smith trans.) (1806) (available online: http://rb.gy/8914ut)—Trans.]

Sittenlehre; an ethics that was supposed to find its highest expression in the construction of the State? For the realization of the community of 'I's, the 'great bourgeois' Spirit demanded a State that turned *all* the powers of labour to that end, and that would exist as the real Order according to which 'a nation sets out wanting to work in common to achieve its happiness' (Hegel). It is only because they were turned to that end that those powers could overcome the current state of alienation. How has one fallen from the absolutism of imperatives to the empiricism of *Zivilization*, from the idea of Constitution-*Verfassung*, as a definition of inviolable and universal values, to juridical positivism, to the idea of the State as a mere juridical order, a guarantor of contracts? Here, an irreparable rupture appears to have taken place: those powers of the *acting* human intellect are 'systematized' [*messe in sistema*] by private interests, or look to the State as a terrain of conquest. The revolutionary idea from which Fichte's idealism sets forth consisted in conceiving of the Political—and its product par excellence, the State—as the highest form of labour in general; the form in which the 'I', expressing itself in its intrinsic intersubjectivity, frees itself of all authority or exterior power. The relation between labour and profession, on the one hand, and with State organization, that is, the Political, on the other, seems to have lost all vital meaning [*senso vitale*], appearing at best to be the effect of a compromise, a calculation, an expedient, so that the bourgeois needs a rationally organized political system merely so as to be adequately *protected* by it. And the Political, in turn, is forced to recognize that the system of social production realized by the bourgeois spirit, and that asserts itself globally today, now constitutes the fundamental pivot of its own authority, stability and duration.

Mann believes, or fools himself into believing, that there continues to exist a bourgeois spirit capable of transforming the Political in the direction of a System of Freedom. For Weber, on the other hand, the only problem that can be realistically confronted is that of a possible relationship between *productive labour*, *the enterprise* and the *social brain*, on the one hand, and *Government*, on the other. For Mann, the bourgeois spirit can still *count* [*valere*] in the full sense of the term. For Weber, it means nothing but profession, technology, responsibility in the epoch of 'accomplished sinfulness'.[14] The Goethean figures of renunciation and resignation prefigure similar outcomes. Between them and Weber comes the transformation of the bourgeois spirit into *capitalism*. This passage, that Weber grasps and suffers from, the artist Mann does not want to see. Overcoming the non-politicality of the bourgeois is certainly necessary for both. But while the former, Weber, is well aware that today it is a case of convincing the now *capitalist* bourgeois Republic and democracy (and its consubstantial adversary: the workers' movement, tearing it from the siren calls of socialism and revolution)[15] by emancipating them from the illusion of being able to carry out their task safely under the *shadow of State power*. The latter, Mann, still thinks, dreams, of a bourgeois 'writ large', capable of infusing the soul of its ethics into the 'body' of the democratic system. The former thinks of the process of globalization as a social system of capitalist production, while the latter thinks of *Weltbürgertum*, of the 'great bourgeois' cosmopolitanism of the era of Kant and Goethe. Mann forces himself to think in terms of continuity and conservation. Weber thinks of the contemporary history of western *Rationalisierung* according to two 'figures' of Spirit that are by now irreconcilable: the Faust of the 'progressive bourgeoisie', the philanthropic Faust, *liberator* of humanity from every form of material or spiritual dependency on the one hand, and, on the other, the Faust that *puts the world to work*, the Faust of universal *Machenschaft*, that abstracts from every End that cannot be pursued by the immanent rationality of the technical-economic system. The Faust of the 'great

14 How might Fichte's expression be translated into Weberian language? Perhaps with *Anpassung*: adaptation to the world, complete alienation into a profession without a vocation, the loss of the sense of the *passion* for truth and justice.

15 See the important lecture Weber gave in Vienna in June 1918, 'Socialism', the Italian edition of which also contains my essay, 'Weber e la critica della ragione socialista' in Max Weber, *Il socialismo reale* (Maurizio Ciampa ed.) (Rome: Savelli 1979). [An English translation of Weber's 'Socialism' can be found in Max Weber's *Political Writings*—Trans.]

transformation' of the nineteenth century could still appear in the form of *ambiguity*. But the *belle époque* already represents the epoch that resolves it, demonstrating its intrinsic aporia and, in the end, its radical ineffectiveness. When Weber speaks of the professions, he now *sees* intellectual labour organized within the system of capitalist production, dominated by the Faust *of capitalism*, even though in its form an active memory of those elements of absolute dedication to labour that characterized the original *Beruf* persist. He wants to convince reactionaries and revolutionaries that only as part of such a system can professional labour remain productive and so will *count* [*varrà*]. The ethical principles are in no way negated but are transposed inexorably onto the terrain of the capitalist *social system* of production. And the Political must *respond* to the interests that determine it and move the latter if it wants to continue to *count* [*valere*].

The bourgeois spirit[16] is a memory that progressively dissolves and exhausts itself in the spirit of capitalism. Weber recognizes this bitterly. Mann persists in thinking that the crisis of that original *liberatory* bourgeois ethics constitutes simply a *Zwischenfall* and that one can escape from its crisis by *remembering*, *bringing to the heart* of Europe the Novalises and Goethes, finally reconciling them with the Whitmans, and that the System of Freedom of a Fichte resounds analogously to 'America Singing',[17] that the Novalis of *Christenheit oder Europa* need not tear down its bridges to the Principles of 1789. None of these great illusions can be found in Weber. But Weber would have been careful not to consider them to be the naive or blind hopes of a literary figure. While being unable to share in them in any way, he could not but painfully feel their *pathos* and certainly he recognized their nobility, their *nobility of spirit*. Moreover, when he outlines the figure of politics, of

---

16 On the different modes of this 'spirit' in literature, in particular, see Franco Moretti's excellent *The Bourgeois: Between History and Literature* (London: Verso, 2013).

17 The reference is almost certainly to Walt Whitman's 'I Hear America Singing'. [Trans.]

praxis, as a profession, precisely in the classical sense (not as a mere job, not mere will to power, nor in contrast as pure conviction, nor as simple *phronesis*, the prudence that experience teaches), he intends to reclaim its *autonomy*—an autonomy that Mann's ethical discourse also sought to affirm. Of course, for such autonomy to have weight and value, it is necessary for it to not pretend to be 'sovereign'. It is necessary that it show itself to be responsible in relation to the power of intellectual-productive labour. However, only in it, if it were possible to defend it, and in the practical *philosophy* that represents it, can 'great bourgeois' ethical values find refuge. Instead, the universal system of labour, the contemporary social brain seems, rather, in all its aspects, to be integrated into capitalist social relations of production. The 'iron cage' essentially means this: that the *creativity* of labour (in the considerations of Mann's *Reflections*: the *genius* able to join intellect and exactitude) appears today to be only able to express itself within that system and dominated by its logic.

If the political is unable to defend its autonomy other than *relative* to its own needs (and thus never deluding itself that it can dominate them), it can and must represent that dimension of the ethics of the professions, irreducible to economic calculation and to the rationale of commercial exchange. Hence, the 'iron cage' is the welding together of profession, Political, and economic 'legality', where the profession becomes merely labour commanded by the system, while maintaining the appearance of *Beruf*. And the Political, for its part, is reduced to the administration of the relation between this labour and the anonymous sovereignty of the Technological-economic, a sovereignty that assumes the mask of a 'law of nature' and presumes to impose itself in such a form everywhere. The obedience to a Nomos that does not presume to be a *factum*, an artifice. Were these to be definitively soldered together, we would then be in a 'polar night'. (What 'lies before us is not the "summer's Front" but, initially at least, a polar night of icy darkness and harshness, whichever group may outwardly turn out the victor.'[18] The

18 Weber, 'Science as a Vocation', p. 93.

symbol of the 'polar night' is a recurrent one in the mythologies of the Munich circles that Schmitt frequents, as well as the George-Kreis.)

But it is nowhere written that this must happen. Of course, the productive, intellectual and political forces are unmistakably developing in this direction. However, one must beware of allowing oneself to be spellbound by the *pathos* of pessimism, even though Schmitt recounts having seen Weber *dying of desperation* in 1920.[19] These very same lectures on intellectual labour exhibit the lines of resistance, the counter-tendencies that Weber believed were possible. By allying with the Political, *politicizing* itself without losing its *ethos*, productive intellectual labour still could, for him, elude Technical-economic hegemony. Thereby, the professions could refuse obtusely accepting the present state. At the same time, in this reciprocal recognition, the Political might have been able to overcome that simply technical-administrative dimension to which capitalist logic always tends to relegate it. In breaking the chain with which science as a profession was shackled to capitalist development, the Political gave consistency and vitality back to the ethics of responsibility understood as the general orientation of existence—beyond the illusion of a great bourgeoisie capable of informing the democratic Republic of its values, and thus capable also of informing an enduring compromise with what the twentieth century called the workers' movement. The duty of the Political had been to combat the servile adaptation to the inevitable appropriation of the products of the social body, of the intelligence of

---

19 'I still reflect upon F. de Vitoria [. . .] Then, for entire days, the impatience of justice assails me; this is the form of desperation involved in my profession of jurist. But I do not want to die from it, as did poor Max Weber, who I saw dying of desperation in 1920. It seemed me then a folly to allow oneself to be consumed in that way, literally disappearing. I now understand the warning, that in the meantime has expired.' Carl Schmitt, *Glossario* (Petra dal Santo ed.) (Milan: Giuffrè, 2001), p. 242. If one fails to grasp the drama between Nomos and Justice *lived* by these great thinkers, it will also be difficult to grasp the 'scientific' aspects of their work . . . I point the reader in the direction of my 'Destino di Dike' in Massimo Cacciari and Natalino Irti, *Elogio del diritto* (with an essay by Werner Jaeger) (Milan: La nave di Teseo, 2019).

the species by the 'laws' of capitalist reproduction. Social science, on its part, while distancing itself from all presumption to being endowed with 'prophetic spirit', and fighting the ideologies of destiny *à la* Spengler, showed itself capable of drawing from the study of the regularities of the historical process fertile indications on what form of the Political might turn out to cohere with the end of *contra-dicting* the subordination of human intellectual labour and the private appropriation of wealth derived from it, without thereby putting a break on or blocking the mechanisms of development. Of course, the Political that pretends to an abstract *freedom* for labour, that is nostalgic for the original ethics of the professions, will lose itself. The witches' sabbath cannot be halted.[20] It would be best to be soberly despairing on this. Nevertheless, there is no logic that prohibits the product of the now globally cooperating species' intelligence, taking place within its indefinite advance, as a historically determined end, to cease being *commanded* by 'laws' that are foreign to all ideas of freedom. But the Political is necessary to *really* conceive such a critique, so that it might be configured as praxis, project and organization. But will the Political be able to incarnate it in the form in which Weber still represents it, that is, within the limits of the modern State, of the modern idea of sovereign statehood? Or, if the end is that of constructing an authentic *contradiction* with respect to the capitalist Faust, does not a Political beyond the State appear necessary?[21]

---

20 'One day, speaking with Max Weber of future prospects, this question arose: when will the witches dance that humanity stages in capitalist countries since the start of the twentieth century end? He answered: when the last ton of iron is fused with the final ton of coal.' Werner Sombart, *Il capitalismo moderno* [*Der moderne Kapitalismus*] (Alessandro Cavalli ed.) (Turin: UTET, 1967), p. 853. How would Weber reply today? I do not think he would refer to the *physical* limits of development, understood in determinist manner. The dance of the witches has revealed its full nature, which is entirely immaterial or *metaphysical*. It unfolds entirely on the terrain of the *power of the mind* and, hence, of the *labour of spirit*.

21 The debate on the (supposed?) twilight of the state-form is now vast, but I would like to recall the 'inaugural' seminar, held in Padua on this theme, to which Gianfranco Miglio, Pierangelo Schiera, Mario Tronti, Giacomo Marramao, Carlo

On this, Weber remains silent. And his democratic Republic, not only the Mannian 'noble' one, shows its historical limits. And yet, up to this meridian, the destiny that he indicated with tragic lucidity continues to admonish us. If, as Benjamin said, the exposing of the past forces us to speak of ourselves, never has this been truer than in the work of Max Weber.

Galli and others participated: Giuseppe Duso (ed.), *La politica oltre lo Stato: Carl Schmitt* (Venice: Arsenale Cooperativa Editrice, 1981).

V

THE END (OF THE END) OF HISTORY

It has made of itself a World[1]—or perhaps should one say *aequor*, a liquid expanse without apparent borders, the ideal dominion of *pirates*? What sovereignty could restrain them? Or is it now only they who 'monitor and punish'? Is it perhaps a case of the World that our poet most loved by Schopenhauer and Nietzsche called 'lauder and tutor of all false virtues, detractor and persecutor of all true ones . . . adversary of all greatness intrinsic and proper to Man; despiser of all high sentiment . . . slave to the strong, tyrannical over the weak, hater of the unhappy'?[2] This is a question that the anguished 'great bourgeois' never ceases to ask itself. In contrast, the spirit of capitalism experiences reality with simple, 'kindly' indifference. Certainly, it is not a reality that is internally resolved, pacified. The World is one, but it is composed of energies that contradict and combat one another. Everything converges in one and everything fragments. The universal affirmation of that spirit does not bear with it any recognition of a political or ethical nature (no longer does the Hegelian *Anerkennung* constitute its End), even less the possibility of any sort of *global* government. When it was still hegemonic, the State-form could represent the space wherein to organize the accord, at least in the form of the contract, between the economic-financial powers and the principles of representative democracy. This was a compromise

1 'Then the earth has become small, and on it hops the last human being . . . His kind is ineradicable, like the flea beetle.' Friedrich Nietzsche, *Thus Spake Zarathustra* (Adrian Del Caro and Robert Pippin ed., Del Caro trans.) (Cambridge: Cambridge University Press, 2006), pp. 9–10. Regarding the 'last man', see my *L'Arcipelago* (Milan: Adelphi, 1997).

2 Giacomo Leopardi, *Pensieri*, LXXXIV.

that might even safeguard a *relative autonomy* of the *Geistige Arbeit*, of the 'labour of spirit'. Hence, the erosion of the nation-state must also be considered as the first cause of the crisis faced by such an autonomy.

The process of globalization (which has nothing to do with a *reductio ad Unum* and even less with the end of social and political conflict) is entirely capitalist and in no way bourgeois. Indeed, the cover provided by national rootedness continued to be a substantial element of *Kulturbürgertum*. The cosmopolitan perspective itself was here conceived of as the 'logical' development of the idea of the nation in terms of *universal individuality*. Yes, Weber's parliament-and-government is called upon to bring into accord, on the principle of (reciprocal) responsibility, the pure globalization of capitalist enterprise with the representation of the plurality of interests and values that *life* ceaselessly throws up. And yet, such representation does not appear politically conceivable or organizable if not on a national basis. It is still upon the 'conservation' of a ('maternal'!) form of national *Gemeinschaft* that also defines a ('paternal'!) global *Gesellschaft*. But now the 'fourth dimension' of the Globe comes into contradiction with the three-dimensional metrics of the state. The increasingly contracted *time* of the Economic and of Technology is unreconciled with the territorial space of political representation. The latter still belongs to the bourgeois form of the spirit of capitalism, as well as to the *culture of the workers' movement*, and to their conflict. Liberal *Kulturbürgertum* and *Sozialismus* experience the same destiny. They stand and fall together. In the end, the *konservative Revolution* had understood this perfectly. And it is precisely when they cease to in-comprehend [*fra-intendersi*][3] themselves that Western representative democracy goes into crisis.

---

3 This play on words is untranslatable: *fra-intendersi* is made up of the prefix *fra-*, 'between', 'among', 'betwixt', and *intendersi*, from the infinitive of 'understand', *intendere*, and the suffix *-si* that is used with the infinitive to derive reflexive third-person object forms. So *fra-intendersi* means 'to misunderstand one another', with the hyphenation (added by the author) drawing attention to the between-ness of the understanding that is 'missed'—to be *within* a relation of in-comprehension. [Trans.]

The Weberian polytheism of values does not have a vulgarly relativistic meaning. It implies the need to confer order on contingency, to methodically organize the contradictions that threaten to explode, recognizing the *limits* that the two fundamental forms of the *geistige Arbeit* reciprocally impose upon one another.[4] This order can only be pursued by *representing* conflict. If this is not posed in the *form* of representativeness [*rappresentanza*], it is destined to be transformed into a self-destructive tumult. But the *value* of representativeness [*rappresentanza*], the secularization of weighty theological traditions is, in the Modern, quintessentially bourgeois. It is born of the repulsion of all pre-established hierarchy and culminates with the democratic consciousness of the irrepressibility of the polytheism of values. The crisis of representative democracy coincides with the extinguishing of the bourgeois spirit.[5] In this spirit, the system of representativeness [*rappresentanza*] itself demanded that a compromise between *maior pars* (greater part) and *sanior pars* (sounder part) would always be possible.[6] That is to say, political action would always be capable of 'overcoming' the opinions and urges of the majority, 'comprehending' them within itself and governing its irrepressible irrational dimension. If it is certainly necessary to think that political classes formed only by the competent is an empty utopia, it nevertheless appears indispensable for there to be a 'professionally' responsible government that democratic procedures should do all they can to favour the selection of the 'best'. Present disillusionment, the disenchantment around this possibility, can already be read in sil-

---

4 Schmitt's 'concept of the Political', the friend-enemy *polemos*, is a *principle of order* designed to essentially determine the relation between sovereign spaces and to *drive out the anguish for the Indeterminate*. It is the opposite of something 'bellicose', as it continues to be represented.

5 The literature on the subject is vast, but only that which confronts the argument with *realism*, at 'the school' of the Machiavellis and Webers, is valuable. In that sense, Danilo Zolo's *Il principato democratico* (Milan: Feltrinelli, 1992) remains a fundamental text.

6 See the classic short text by Edoardo Ruffini, *Il principio maggioritario* (Milan: Adelphi, 1976).

houette in Weber's pages—and in the irony, almost, with which Schumpeter, in his classic *Capitalism, Socialism and Democracy* (1942), treats the 'imperatives' to which democracy supposedly conforms during its evolution (from the intellectual capacities of the representatives as much as the represented, to the open and dynamic character of the bureaucratic apparatuses) *without it ever doing so*. Schumpeter ruthlessly reveals the implicit *ought-to-be* [*dover-essere*] with which Weber's thinking is laden.

Nevertheless, the 'quality' of political action does not depend on subjective causes. It depends upon the capitalist form of the current globalization (in contrast to the first form that straddled the nineteenth and twentieth centuries, when supremacy remained in the hands of the bourgeoisie and the nation-states), on the crisis of the space of statehood and the forms of representation that it alone rendered possible; it depends upon the end of the bourgeois spirit that in those spaces and in those forms in which it recognized itself, only after a strenuous labour. The more the effective power of the Political is reduced, the more the demagogic-plebiscitary component grows within its institutions. The crisis of representativeness [*rappresentanza*] accompanies the spread of the idea of the possibility of the *identification* of Government and public opinion. The recognition of social complexity that underpins democratic polytheism disappears in the myth of the People. And the People *im-mediately* make demands upon the Leader, that is, it requires that he proclaim: I am your Leader and so *I follow you*. The crisis of representativity, therefore, becomes the crisis of all other elements and functions that *mediate* civil society and Government, not only all the 'intermediary bodies' (associations, trade unions, etc.), but also those essential functions of the state that are not *im-mediate* expressions of the *maior pars*, as in the case of the judiciary. At a certain point it is inevitable that the 'corruption' of political authority spreads to 'corrupting' the technical-administrative-bureaucratic apparatuses that form the structure of the modern state—in short, that they cease to *function*. In the best-case scenario, one will have the law-abiding functionary, following the letter of the norms and incapable of initiative, what Schmitt in his early *Das Wert des Staates und die Bedeutung des Einzelnen* (The value of the state and the significance of the individual) called '*Pflichtwicht*', the 'duty gnome' [*doverante*].[7] The more the effective capacity of the Politician to be authentically *responsible*, of responding to the complexity of interests and questions of civil society, is eroded, the more are these tendencies destined to reinforce themselves. And the more there bursts onto the scene of the Political an incompetent multitude that varnishes with political identities, vague nebulous passions, hatreds, desires, frustrations and resentments—here speaks Gramsci, not only Weber.

Then there reappears on the scene, in an almost tragicomic key, the critique of bourgeois spirit as the neutralization of the Political. No one, certainly, would say with Feuerbach that 'politics must become our religion',[8] but the intolerance for mediation that is implicit in the form of representativity [*rappresentanza*] in the name of the efficacy of political command presents itself again in the most varied and incidental forms. Only that now it is the image of pure *impotence*. The bourgeois spirit is not defeated by nostalgia for the Sovereign but rather the reverse, by the uprooting cosmopolitanism of the Economic—and it has suffered such

7 See Carl Schmitt, *Der Wert des Staates und die Bedeutung des Einzelnen* (Berlin: Duncker & Humblot, 2004), p. 92. An English translation is available in 'The Value of the State and the Significance of the Individual' in *Carl Schmitt's Early Legal-Theoretical Writings*, p. 222. The Italian *doverante*, while potentially disparaging, suggests simply a dutiful individual. The sentence in Schmitt from which this contemptuous term appears—drawn from Theodor Däubler's colossal epic poem 'The Northern Light'—reads as follows: 'What is contemptible in a subaltern pettiness and pedantry, in the "duty gnomes" (Däubler), is precisely the incapacity to become one with a great matter, the incapacity for abstraction, and the consequent confusion of what is here referred to as the state and its task with the "higher administrative agency" and the concrete humans who are its organs.' [Trans.]

8 We can find this cited in Frederick Engels, 'Ludwig Feuerbach and the End of Classical German Philosophy' in *Marx & Engels Collected Works*, VOL. 26 (London: Lawrence and Wishart, 1990), p. 378. [Trans.]

a defeat for some time. There is no 'political religion' that has ended democratic polytheism. This end is decreed by *capitalism as religion*,[9] which is entirely indifferent to the empty declarations about the loss of state sovereignty and, in its principles, is entirely consistent with the dismantling of all mediatory powers. Sovereignism [*sovranismo*][10] might itself be understood as an important ideological dimension of the capitalist World and its religious essence. Such a dimension is even more significant the more unwitting it is, functioning as cover and containment that Schumpeter had already considered essential to the government of

---

9 Recently, there has been a wealth of interpretations of Benjamin's 1921 fragment, 'Capitalism as Religion', composed at the same time as the 'Theologico-Political Fragment'. The Italian versions are many and discordant, from that by Gianfranco Bonola and Michele Ranchetti in Walter Benjamin, *Sul concetto della storia* (Turin: Einaudi, 1997), to that contained in *Il culto del capitale* (Macerata: Quodlibet, 2014) [Available in English in Walter Benjamin, *Selected Writings*, VOL. 1 (Marcus Bullock and Michael W. Jennings eds) (Cambridge, MA: Harvard University Press, 2004), pp. 288–89.] The capitalist 'cult' consists precisely in the exclusion of all Ends, that is, in wanting to be *in-finitely* celebrated, without respite or 'pity' (recall Fichte's unbridled sinfulness). It demands that all be *in-debted* to it (all captured in the web of the cycle of money-through-money, that is, precisely *debt*, where all are 'guilty'). Benjamin's fragment is certainly fundamental but, in order for it not to give way to abstract theologico-philosophical ruminations, it must be related back to its historical-political, economic and juridical context, to those same Benjaminian essays on the debacle of the bourgeoisie, on the one hand (in this regard, his introduction to the letters of the 'great bourgeois' collected in *German Men and Women* from 1936, counterpart to the aforementioned *Vom Weltbürger zum Grossbürger*); and, naturally, to Marx's analysis of the character of the 'transcendence' of the thing in its commodity form, on the other.

10 This term is much more common in Italian (and French, *souverainisme*) to highlight—ironically—what is much more clearly represented in the anglophone contexts of 'Brexit' and 'America First': that is, the idea of 'taking back control' from alien forces, which could be supranational bodies such as the European Union, international law, or from unwanted 'illegal' 'aliens'. [Trans.]

the 'natural' tyranny of processes of innovation in all fields that so characterizes the dominant social system of production.[11]

Can Political labour no longer appear as *geistige Arbeit*? Perhaps. However, its twilight in no way coincides with that of *intellectual labour* in general. How have Marx and Weber understood the latter? Just as complex, socially organized productive labour? Certainly not. Marx has 'burrowed' into its form and from it he thought he had drawn a subject that incarnated that System of Freedom of early revolutionary idealism, to which he always harked back, if not always wittingly. Weber found in the idea of *Beruf* an immanent political intentionality, he 'invoked' its commitment, its participation in the democratic game. In other words, they both saw in the *Geist* immanent to *geistige Arbeit* the real possibility, if not of overcoming, of contesting the 'iron cage' represented by the dependent, *alienated* form of labour. Both, in very different ways, have denied that is in the *nature* of intellectual, scientific and technical labour be *subordinated* to the Political and to the Economic, or to their *closed* system. It is not the destiny of the *geistige Arbeit* to be subsumed by the technological-economic system. In what ways, in what timeframes might the 'labour of spirit' emerge and count as a truly autonomous energy and, thereby, represent itself as a 'science'—always in essence that of Epimetheus[12]—it will never be able to say. However, it is possible to investigate and together know the set of circumstances that render the assertion of such a demand conceivable. And to now grasp that any form of *autonomy* of the Political, if this were ever to occur in the epoch of globalized capitalism, can only found itself upon the self-liberating power of intellectual labour, that is, as a representation and order that finds in such power both its motive cause and its final cause.

---

11 Ultimately, one could read, as Löwith attempted, the Hegelian state itself as a 'great form' of containment or *katechon against* the eruption 'from below' of revolutionary energies destructive of the idea of representation.

12 That is to say, a kind of hindsight, taking place after the fact, like the owl of Minerva's flight at dusk. [Trans.]

The 'end of history'[13] is only conceivable in two forms (when it is not apocalyptic mythology, which often hides only the fear for the end of the 'private' world).[14] Either in the form of a purely affirmative 'absolute knowing' that subsumes every tradition and itself generates that Kingdom where *it is known* a priori how every interrogation must be posed and where the unknown is nothing but the knowable. Or in the form of an insistence within contradiction without there being any End that one can indicate. The history of negation (which is the history of *historical humanity*) thus continues without ever encountering that negation of the negation, constituted by 'absolute knowing'—and yet, the moment of the negative exhausts itself in being posed. It does not engender any *Auf-hebung*, nor does it contain the image of any end that overcomes its immediate givenness. In this sense, the 'end of history' is nothing but the *non-transcendability* of historical becoming. The being-there [*esserci*] that becomes solely historical is the being-there of the 'end of history'. History is only given as long as being-there [*esserci*] is understood ek-statically,[15] as a *task* directed to an end, and when that end assumes at each point a determinate shape. If the simple form of indefinite becoming no longer presents anything *beyond* itself, it ends up annihilating the historicity of being-there itself.

---

13 I do not believe that the concept of the 'end of history' developed by Kojève in his overly mythologized *Introduction to the Reading of Hegel* can be summarized in the inevitable idea, the destined overturning of the sense of history inaugurated by a God who becomes man in the Man alone without God—an overturning that concludes with the assertion of the universal and homogeneous *Imperium*, capable of subsuming within itself all *particularity*, hence those of the state and the Church themselves. Such an 'end' only takes place in the *acceleration* of times, not at the end of times. The time of the end of history is that of the acceleration without end, of the *in-finite* advance of the definitive victory of becoming over all 'substance'.

14 See Ernesto de Martino, *The End of the World: Cultural Apocalypse and Transcendence* (Dorothy Louise Zinn trans.) (Chicago: University of Chicago Press, 2023).

15 The notion of the '*Ekstase*', of the ek-static, also in Heidegger's sense, plays on the etymological Greek meaning of the term as 'standing outside' (see Heidegger, *Being and Time*, p. 377n2). [Trans.]

Despite all we have said, the form of the *geistige Arbeit*, for Weber still operating in the idea of the professions and, in Marx, still germinating within commanded labour itself, represents for them both, in a kind of dissenting accord, the real possibility of the arising of a *negative* that brings indefinite becoming to an *end*. They both know that the Christian *time-that-is-missing* has dilated immeasurably, it too has become *masslos*, to the point that all idea of an End or an Eschaton has foundered. No one awaits the *Parousia* or Day of the Lord anymore. However, the *analysis* of actual reality demonstrates that the catastrophe *is* in every instance, within the powers or archons of this world and their *polemos*. The 'labour of spirit' is that which in every *crisis* sees the sign of the intrinsic unfoundedness of the dominion of *apeiron's* measureless continuity of becoming. The 'labour of spirit' inhabits time in light of the ends that can break its web—and, within such a light, can *negate* those powers and archons who structure their Auctoritas on indefinite becoming. The end (of the end) of history cannot, therefore, be made to coincide with the end of history, since it is from within its current configuration that can mature the energy capable of imposing a new *end* to becoming, that is, one capable of interpreting it and performing it ek-statically. Those who fail to note this *final* possible horizon of Weberian disenchantment belong inexorably to the worst species [*genia*] of the bewitched [*incantati*], those of the disenchanted [*disincantati*] heralds of destiny.

Bibliography

Asor Rosa, Alberto. *Le armi della critica*. Turin: Einaudi, 2011.

Asor Rosa, Alberto. *Thomas Mann o dell'ambiguità borghese*. Bari: De Donato, 1971.

Benjamin, Walter. 'Capitalism as Religion' in *Selected Writings*, vol. 1 (Marcus Bullock and Michael W. Jennings eds). Cambridge, MA: Harvard University Press, 2004.

Benjamin, Walter. 'Die Jugend schwieg' in *Gesammelte Schriften*, vol. 2, part 1 (Rolf Tiedemann and H. Schweppenhäuser eds). Frankfurt am Main: Suhrkamp, 1972.

Benjamin, Walter. 'Die Jugend schwieg'. *Die Aktion* 3(42) (18 October 1913): coll. 979–981.

Benjamin, Walter. *Il culto del capitale*. Macerata: Quodlibet, 2014.

Bevilacqua, Giuseppe. *Letteratura e società nel secondo Reich*. Milan: Longanesi, 1977.

Benjamin, Walter. 'Metafisica della gioventù' in *Metafisica della gioventù: Scritti 1910–1918* (Giorgio Agamben ed.), Opere di Walter Benjamin, vol. 1. Turin: Einaudi, 1982.

Benjamin, Walter. *Sul concetto della storia*. Turin: Einaudi, 1997.

Breuer, Stefan. *Anatomie der Konservativen Revolution*. Darmstadt: Wissenschaftliche Buchgesellschaft, 1993.

Bruer, Stefan. 'Between "Conservative Revolution", Aesthetic Fundamentalism and New Nationalism: Thomas Mann's Early Political Writings'. *History of the Human Sciences* 11(2) (1998): 1–23.

Cacciari, Massimo. 'Destino di Dike' in Massimo Cacciari and Natalino Irti, *Elogio del diritto* (with an essay by Werner Jaeger). Milan: La nave di Teseo, 2019.

Cacciari, Massimo. 'Grandezza e tramonto dell'utopia' in Massimo Cacciari and Paolo Prodi, *Occidente senza utopie*. Bologna: Il Mulino, 2016.

Cacciari, Massimo. *Hamletics* (Matteo Mandarini trans.). London: Seagull Books, 2023.

CACCIARI, Massimo. Introduction to Georg Simmel, *Diario postumo*. Turin: Aragno, 2011.

CACCIARI, Massimo. *Krisis: Saggio sulla crisi del pensiero negativo da Nietzsche a Wittgenstein*. Milan: Feltrinelli, 1976.

CACCIARI, Massimo. *L'Arcipelago*. Milan: Adelphi, 1997.

CACCIARI, Massimo. *La mente inquieta: Saggio sull'Umanesimo*. Turin: Einaudi, 2019.

CACCIARI, Massimo. *Pensiero negativo e razionalizzazione*. Venice: Marsilio, 1977.

CACCIARI, Massimo. *Walter Rathenau e il suo ambiente*. Bari: De Donato, 1979.

CACCIARI, Massimo. 'Weber e la critica della ragione socialista' in Max Weber, *Il socialismo reale* (Maurizio Ciampa). Rome: Savelli, 1979.

CACCIARI, Massimo. *The Withholding Power: An Essay on Political Theology* (Edi Pucci trans., Howard Caygill intro.). London: Bloomsbury, 2018.

CARRINO, Agostino. *L'irrazionale nel concetto: Comunità e diritto in Emil Lask*. Naples: Edizioni scientifiche italiane, 1983.

CASSIN, Barbara, Emily Apter, Jacques Lezra, and Michael Wood (eds). *Dictionary of Untranslatables: A Philosophical Lexicon*. Princeton, NJ: Princeton University Press, 2014.

CASSIRER, Ernst. 'The Idea of a Republican Constitution' (Seth Berk trans.). *The Philosophical Forum* 49 (2018): 3–17.

CESA, Claudio. *J. G. Fichte e l'idealismo trascendentale*. Bologna: Il Mulino, 1992.

DE GIOVANNI, Biagio. *Libertà e vitalità: Benedetto Croce e la crisi della coscienza europea*. Bologna: Il Mulino, 2018.

DE MARTINO, Ernesto. *The End of the World: Cultural Apocalypse and Transcendence* (Dorothy Louise Zinn trans.). Chicago: University of Chicago Press, 2023.

DUMONT, Louis. *Homo aequalis* (Guido Viale trans.). Milan: Adelphi, 2019.

DUMONT, Louis. *Homo Hierarchicus* (Mark Sainsbury trans.). Chicago, IL: University of Chicago Press, 1970.

DUSO, Giuseppe (ed.). *La politica oltre lo Stato: Carl Schmitt*. Venice: Arsenale Cooperativa Editrice, 1981.

ENGELS, Frederick. 'Ludwig Feuerbach and the End of Classical German Philosophy' in *Marx & Engels Collected Works*, VOL. 26. London: Lawrence and Wishart, 1990.

ESPOSITO, Roberto. *Two: The Machine of Political Theology and the Place of Thought* (Zakiya Hanafi trans.). New York: Fordham University Press, 2015.

Fichte, Johann Gottlieb. *Contribution to the Correction of the Public's Judgement on the French Revolution of 1793* (Jeffrey Church and Anna Maria Schön trans). New York: SUNY Press, 2021.

Fichte, Johann Gottlieb. 'Lecture I: The Absolute Vocation of Man' in *The Vocation of the Scholar* (William Smith trans.). London: John Chapman, 1848.

Freund, Julien. *La crisi dello Stato tra decisione e norma* (Agostino Carrino ed.). Naples: Leviathan, 2008.

Gastaldi, Ugo. 'Max Weber tra protestantismo e capitalismo' in *Protestantismo e capitalismo*. Turin: Claudiana, 1983.

Hegel, Georg Wilhelm Friedrich. *Elements of the Philosophy of Right* (Allen W. Wood. ed., H. B. Nisbet trans.). Cambridge: Cambridge University Press, 1991.

Hegel, Georg Wilhelm Friedrich. *The Phenomenology of Spirit* (Terry Pinkard trans.). Cambridge: Cambridge University Press, 2018.

Heidegger, Martin. *The Question Concerning Technology and Other Writings* (William Lovitt trans.). New York: Harper Torchbooks, 1977.

Hobsbawm, Eric. *The Age of Capital 1848–1875*. London: Abacus, 1988.

Hofmannsthal, Hugo von. 'The Written Word as the Spiritual Space of the Nation' in *Hugo von Hofmannsthal and the Austrian Idea: Selected Essays and Addresses 1906–1927* (David S. Luft ed. and trans.). West Lafayette, IN: Purdue University Press, 2011.

Irti, Natalino. *L'età della decodificazione*. Milan: Giuffrè, 1999.

Irti, Natalino. *Un diritto incalcolabile*. Turin: Giappichelli, 2016.

Ivaldo, Marco. *Libertà e ragione: L'etica di Fichte*. Milan: Ugo Mursia Editore, 1992.

Kierkegaard, Søren. *Purity of Heart Is to Will One Thing* (Douglas V. Steere trans.). New York: Harper Torchbooks, 1956.

Kierkegaard, Søren. *Upbuilding Discourses in Various Spirits* (Howard V. Hong and Edna H. Hong trans). Princeton, NJ: Princeton University Press, 1993.

Koyré, Alexandre. *Études d'histoire de la pensée philosophique*. Paris: Gallimard, 1981.

Löwith, Karl, ed. *La sinistra hegeliana: Testi scelti*. Bari: Laterza, 1960.

Löwith, Karl. *From Hegel to Nietzsche* (D. E. Green trans.). New York: Columbia University Press, 1964.

Luporini, Cesare. 'Fichte e la destinazione del dotto' in *Filosofi vecchi e nuovi*. Florence: Sansoni, 1947.

MANN, Thomas. *Essays of Three Decades* (Helen Tracy Lowe-Porter trans.). New York: Vintage, 1957.

MANN, Thomas. 'Goethe als Repräsentant des bürgerlichen Zeitalters'. *Die Neue Rundschau* 4 (April 1932): 434–462.

MANN, Thomas. *Reflections of a Nonpolitical Man* (W. D. Morris et al. trans.). New York: New York Review of Books, 2021.

MANN, Thomas. *Scritti minori* (Lavinia Mazzucchetti ed.). *Tutte le opere di Thomas Mann*, VOL. 12. Milan: Mondadori, 1958.

MANN, Thomas, and Benedetto Croce. *Carteggio 1930–1936*. Naples: Tolmino, 1999.

MASI, Felice. *Emil Lask: Il pathos della forma*. Macerata: Quodlibet, 2010.

MASSIMILLA, Edoardo. 'Benedetto Croce a Max Weber'. *Archivio di storia della cultura* 29 (2016).

MASSIMILLA, Edoardo. *Presupposti e percorsi del comprendere esplicativo: Max Weber e i suoi interlocutori*. Naples: Liguori, 2014.

MASSIMILLA, Edoardo. *Scienza, professione, gioventù: Rifrazioni weberiane*. Catanzaro: Rubbettino, 2008.

MCCLELLAND, Charles E. 'The Organization of the "Free" Professions: Medicine, Law, Engineering, and Chemistry' in *The German Experience of Professionalization*. Cambridge: Cambridge University Press, 1991.

MIEGGE, Mario, Lilia Carusi Corsani, and Ugo Gastaldi. *Protestantismo e capitalismo da Calvino a Weber*. Turin: Claudiana, 1983.

MIGLIO, Gianfranco. *Le regolarità della politica*, VOL. 2. Milan: Giuffré, 1987.

MORETTI, Franco. *The Bourgeois: Between History and Literature*. London: Verso, 2013.

NIENHAUS, Stefan. *Aurora boreale: Tre studi sugli elementi, lo spirito e l'attualità dell'opera di Theodor Däubler*. Naples: Edizioni scientifiche Italiane, 1995.

NIETZSCHE, Friedrich. *Daybreak* (R. J. Hollingdale trans.). Cambridge: Cambridge University Press, 1997.

NIETZSCHE, Friedrich. *Thus Spake Zarathustra* (Adrian Del Caro and Robert Pippin eds). Cambridge: Cambridge University Press, 2006.

ROSSI, Guido. *Il gioco delle regole*. Milan: Adelphi, 2006.

RUFFINI, Edoardo. *Il principio maggioritario*. Milan: Adelphi, 1976.

SALZ, Arthur. *Für die Wissenschaft: gegen die Gebildeten unter ihren Verächtern*. Munich: Drei Masken, 1921.

SCHMITT, Carl. 'The Age of Neutralizations and Depoliticizations'. *Telos* 96 (1993): 130–142.

SCHMITT, Carl. *Carl Schmitt's Early Legal-Theoretical Writings* (Lars Vinx and Samuel Garrett Zeitlin eds and trans). Cambridge: Cambridge University Press, 2021.

SCHMITT, Carl. *Der Wert des Staates und die Bedeutung des Einzelnen*. Berlin: Duncker & Humblot, 2004.

SCHMITT, Carl. *Ex Captivitate Salus* (Matthew Hannah trans.). Cambridge: Polity Press, 2017.

SCHMITT, Carl. *Glossario* (Petra dal Santo ed.). Milan: Giuffrè, 2001.

SCHMITT, Carl. *The Nomos of the Earth in the International Law of the Jus Publicum Europaeum* (G. L. Ulmen trans.). New York: Telos Press, 2004.

SCHMITT, Carl. *Political Romanticism* (Guy Oakes trans.). Cambridge, MA: MIT Press, 1986.

SCHMITT, Carl. *Theodor Däublers 'Nordlicht': Drei Studien über die Elemente, den Geist und die Aktualità dell'opera*. Munich: Müller, 1916.

SCHWAB, Alexander. 'Beruf und Jugend'. *Die weißen Blätter* 4(5) (May 1917).

SEYFARTH, Constans, and Walter M. Sprondel (eds). *Religion und gesellschaftliche Entwicklung*. Frankfurt am Main: Suhrkamp, 1973.

SIMMEL, Georg. *The Sociology of Georg Simmel* (K. H. Wolff ed. and trans.). Glencoe, IL: The Free Press, 1950.

SOMBART, Werner. *Il capitalismo moderno* (Alessandro Cavalli ed.). Turin: UTET, 1967.

WEBER, Max. *La scienza come professione: La politica come professione* (Massimo Cacciari intro.). Milan: Mondadori, 2006.

WEBER, Max. 'Science as a Vocation' in *The Vocation Lectures* (David Owen and Tracy B. Strong eds, Rodney Livingstone trans.). Indianapolis, IN: Hackett, 2004.

WEBER, Max. 'Zwischen zwei Gesetzen' in *Gesammelte politische Schriften*. Tübingen: Mohr / Siebeck, 1958.

WILAMOWITZ-MOELLENDORFF, Ulrich von. *Cultura classica e crisi tedesca* (Luciano Canfora ed.). Bari: De Donato, 1977.

ZOLO, Danilo. *Il principato democratico*. Milan: Feltrinelli, 1992.